THE SINKING OF THE
TITANIC

The Mystery Solved

THE SINKING OF THE
TITANIC

The Mystery Solved

Captain L.M. Collins

SOUVENIR PRESS

First published in the Canada by Breakwater Books,
St John's, Newfoundland
First published in Great Britain in 2004 by Souvenir Press Ltd
43 Great Russell Street, London WC1B 3PD
This paperback edition 2008

ISBN 9780285638167

Publisher's note: The publishers of the original book and of the present UK edition
have made an exhaustive search to locate the copyright holders of the photographs
included therein. If anyone should have additional information regarding copyright
please contact Breakwater Books Ltd at 00 1 709 722 6680.

Typeset by FiSH Books, London
Printed and bound in Great Britain

THIS BOOK IS dedicated to the memory of my father, the late Captain Frank Collins, who taught me the maxim of good seamanship: when in doubt, never assume, always confirm.

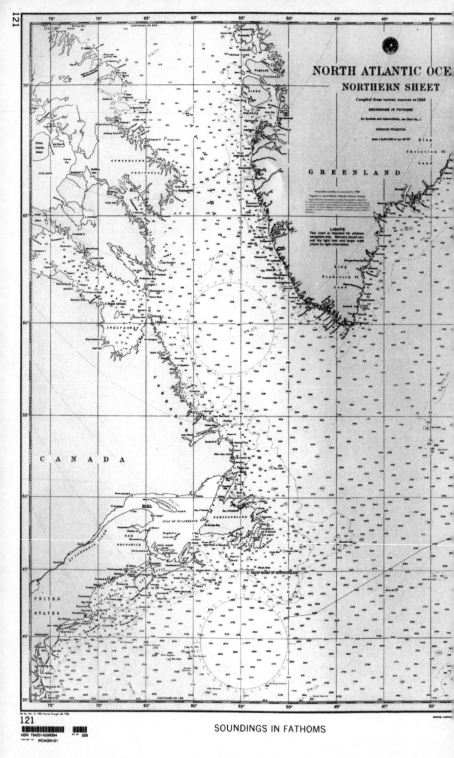

SOUNDINGS IN FATHOMS

Titanic's Great Circle Track

SOUNDINGS IN FATHOMS

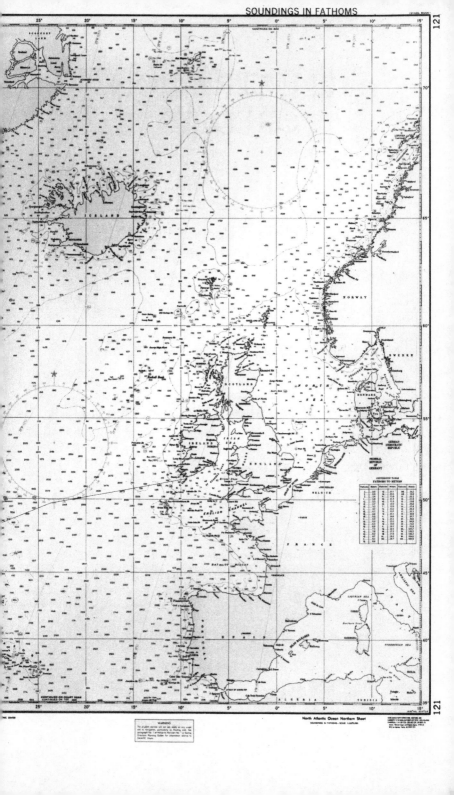

North Atlantic Ocean Northern Sheet
SOUNDINGS IN FATHOMS · SCALE 1:4,875,000

ILLUSTRATION CREDITS

CONTENTS

FOREWORD

I have read with great interest the analysis of the events leading to the sinking of the *Titanic* as related by Captain Collins. I have known Captain Collins for many years and have always appreciated his professionalism, which was particularly evident during his years as a marine pilot. His extensive experience at sea, followed by his many years as a pilot in the waters of Newfoundland, certainly qualify him for this in-depth study of the published causes of the tragic sinking of this magnificent ocean liner. His knowledge of the ice conditions along the coast of his native Canadian province further confirms his expertise and understanding of the dangers that lay in the path of the *Titanic* on that fateful night.

My interest in the *Titanic* began when I was a youngster, as I listened with fascination to my father telling me about the voyage of my grandfather, who, as captain of the Canadian Government ship Montmagny, was sent to the site of the sinking to recover victims of this tragedy. A few photographs taken at the site of the recovery of the last four bodies, as well as a life ring that held one of the victims, were brought home by my grandfather, and they remind me to this day of this sad event.

This new approach to the possible cause of the sinking of the *Titanic* put forward by Captain Collins will, I am sure, stimulate renewed debate as to the real cause of this disaster. Getting to the truth, even after so many years, can still serve as a valuable lesson to us all. For the future we should strive to properly identify the cause of such tragedies if we are to introduce the appropriate corrective measures.

Michel Pouliot, President
International Maritime Pilots' Association
Canadian Marine Pilots' Association (CMSG)

TITANIC:

Aftermath and Prelude

From a calculation... a very light contact was made...
the injury was evidently a very slight one...

— Edward Wilding, naval architect
to Messrs. Harland and Wolff, to
the British enquiry

On April 15, 1912, the world awoke to the news that the RMS *Titanic* had met with disaster some 300 miles off the coast of Newfoundland. As the day wore on, the depth of the tragedy became apparent. The ship had sunk, with an incredible loss of life. Almost 1500 were dead; over 700 plucked from lifeboats after a bone-chilling night on the sea. Courts of inquiry – first in America and then in Great Britain – were quickly convened, witnesses called and examined. Survivors recounted the last harrowing hours, while the experts attempted to explain the seemingly unexplainable. And ever since that time the misinterpretation of the evidence that was given at the courts of inquiry has perpetuated the myth that the *Titanic* collided with an iceberg, towering some 55 to 60 feet above the water.

Because Captain E.J. Smith and the senior officers, with the exception of Second Officer Charles Lightoller – who was off watch and in his cabin – were lost with the ship, no on-bridge professional evidence was available to the courts of inquiry. The only surviving eye witnesses who were actively on deck duty were lookouts, Frederick Fleet and Reginald Lee, in the crow's nest. Fourth Officer Joseph Boxhall and Quartermasters Robert Hitchens, Alfred Olliver, and George Rowe were on watch, but they were not in a position to see exactly what it was the *Titanic* struck. Therefore, only some of their testimony is plausible.

Historians have comprehensively documented the life of the *Titanic* from her inception in the summer of 1907 to 10 p.m., April 14, 1912. The final hours in the life of the ship, however – from 10 p.m. on the 14th to 2:20 a.m. on the 15th – largely remain a matter of conjecture. As such, they provide ample fodder for the armchair theorist.

The RMS *Titanic* was first conceived in mid-1907 by J. Bruce Ismay, chairman and managing director of the White Star Line, and the Right Honourable Lord Pirrie, a partner and managing director of the Harland and Wolff shipyards. She was constructed by the Harland and Wolff shipyard of Belfast, Ireland, under survey of the British Board of Trade, for a passenger certificate and compliance with the American immigration laws. She was licensed to carry 2603 passengers and 944 crew members, a total of 3547 people, only 1178 of whom were assured a place in her 20 lifeboats.

The *Titanic* was the largest ship of her time. She measured 882 feet and 9 inches in length, 92.5 feet in breadth, and 95 feet from the boat deck to her keel. She displaced 51,310 tons with the 45,000 HP generated by the three engines that were designed to give her a top speed of 23 or 24 knots. At the time of the accident, the drop from her boat deck to the water-line was about 60$\frac{1}{2}$ feet.

Her keel was laid on March 22, 1909. Just a little over two years later, on May 31, 1911, she was launched at

12:15 p.m. On April 2, 1912, she left Belfast to undergo her sea trials. From there, she was on to Southampton.

She arrived at Southampton just before midnight, April 3, and docked at berth 44. The next day the onerous tasks of hiring the crew and loading the cargo and coal began. By Sunday, April 7, a total of 4427 tons of coal had been placed on board – an impressive amount, to be sure, but still short of the bunkers' capacity owing to a serious strike by the coal workers of the country. The fresh foods were loaded in the storerooms on Monday, April 8, and the final inspection by the Board of Trade surveyor was completed by Tuesday, April 9. That night, all the officers except Captain Smith took their berths on the *Titanic*.

Captain Smith arrived on board the next morning, Wednesday, April 10, and received the sailing report from Chief Officer Henry Wilde. At 9:30 a.m., the first train, carrying first-, second-, and third-class passengers, arrived from London. At 11 a.m., Pilot George Bowyer boarded, and at 11:45 a.m. the sirens, announcing the *Titanic*'s departure, were heard. By 12:05 p.m. she was ready to sail.

With the pilot in conduct, the *Titanic*'s mooring lines were cast off and the tugs began to move her away from the dock. Before clearing the dock, however, the White Star ship had to pass the liners *Oceanic* and *New York*, which were moored alongside each other at berth 38. Because of the *Titanic*'s volume of displacement and speed in the shallow water of the narrow channel, interaction – the reaction of the ship's hull to pressure exerted on its underwater form – between the ships caused the moored *Oceanic* and *New York* to "range on their moorings" and be pulled away from the wharf. The *Oceanic* escaped mishap when a sixty-foot gangway dropped from the wharf into the water, but the *New York* broke adrift altogether. The only thing that saved the *New York* from crashing into the *Titanic*'s stern was the *Titanic*'s going astern on the port

'Letting-Go The Last Rope' at Southampton

engine to help make the turn into the River Test. The transverse thrust of the port propeller fortunately had the effect of moving the stern to starboard, away from the danger, while the quick-water flow from the propeller lessened the suction effect and created a "wash" between the *Titanic* and the New York. Through the prompt action of a couple of tugs, lines were made fast and the *New York* was moved back alongside the wharf. It was more than an hour later before the *Titanic* steamed out of Southampton harbour, and not until Pilot Bowyer disembarked at the Nab Lightship did she begin the 65-mile crossing of the English Channel and her maiden voyage.

The first stop was Cherbourg, where she arrived at 6:30 p.m. Once passengers had embarked, the *Titanic* set out again, heading this time for Queenstown, Ireland, on a run of 314 miles. Less than a day later, on Thursday,

April 11, at 11:30 a.m. she anchored seven cables off Roche's Point. The tenders Ireland and America delivered passengers and mail to the waiting ship. By 1:30 p.m., the *Titanic* was ready for her transatlantic trek. Weighing anchor at 2 p.m., she set sail for New York. By late afternoon, she was finally heading out to open sea.

The newest and most luxurious ship in the world carried 1316 passengers: 325 first class, 285 second class, and 706 third class. Her crew numbered 892, which consisted of 73 from the deck department, 325 from the engine department, and 494 from the stewards department. The eight bandsmen and the two telegraphists were not employed by the White Star Line. The total number of people on board was 2208.[1] As K.C. Barnaby points out in his book *Some Ship Disasters and their Causes*, she was sailing with little more than half her capacity and how much worse the tragedy would have been had she sailed with a full passenger list![2]

The *Titanic's* navigating staff comprised seven deck officers and Captain Smith. All were certified as master mariners. Like Captain Smith, Chief Officer Wilde, First Officer William Murdoch, Second Officer Lightoller, and Fourth Officer Boxhall held extra master certificates. Third Officer Herbert Pitman, Fifth Officer Harold Lowe, and Sixth Officer James Moody held master foreign-going certificates.

---

1 According to the *Report on the Loss of the S.S. Titanic: The Official Government Enquiry*, p. 70, the *Titanic* at the time of the disaster had 2201 people on board. It is not clear how the enquiry arrived at this number.

2 Barnaby, K.C. *Some Ship Disasters and their Causes*. New Jersey: A.S. Barnes and Company, Inc., 1970, p. 105.

The officers of the *Titanic*.
STANDING, from left to right: Herbert McElroy, Chief Purser; Charles Lightoller, Second Officer; Herbert Pitman, Third Officer; Joseph Boxhall, Fourth Officer; Harold Lowe, Fifth Officer.
SEATED, from left to right: James Moody, Sixth officer; Henry Wilde, Chief Officer; Captain Smith; William Murdoch, First Officer.

Her navigating equipment was the most up-to-date for the era. It consisted of a standard and two steering magnetic compasses, charts and publications, Kelvin's patent sounding machines for finding the depth of water under the ship without having to stop the ship, flash signal lamps above the shelters at each end of the navigating bridge for Morse signalling with other ships, submarine signalling apparatus, sextants, and chronometers. As well, the wireless equipment was the standard equipment that was aboard most 1912 transatlantic passenger liners. The two wireless operators maintained a continuous 24-hour watch, sending messages from passengers and receiving notifications of ice along the Atlantic route.

The first few days out were uneventful. For the most part the weather was fine, which made for a smooth passage. Once the ship had left Queenstown, her speed was "opened up on the long run to New York."[3] The first day's run was 480 miles. On the second day it was 545 miles and on the third, 546. For the last day's run the average speed was more than 22 knots.

Reports of ice had not gone unnoticed. Harold Bride and Jack Phillips, the two Marconi wireless operators, had already received messages that ships eastbound and westbound on the North Atlantic routes were encountering ice between 41° and 42° north latitude and 49° and 50° west longitude. Then, at 9 a.m. on April 14, a wireless message, addressed to Captain Smith from the SS *Coronia*, was received. It read as follows:

> Captain, *Titanic*. – West-bound steamers report bergs, growlers, and field-ice in 42° N. from 49° to 51° W, 12th April. Compliments. – Barr.[4]

Captain Smith acknowledged receipt of the message, which, it must be noted, referred to bergs, growlers, and field ice that was sighted on April 12, two days before the *Titanic's* impact with the ice.

Devotional services were held on board the ship at 10 a.m., and at 12 p.m. the noon position fix was obtained. Her course was then south 62° west true.

---

3   Winocour, Jack, ed. *The Story of the Titanic as Told by Its Survivors Lawrence Beesley, Archibald Gracie, Commander Lightoller, Harold Bride*. New York: Dover Publications, Inc. 1960, p.279.

4   *Report on the Loss of the S.S. Titanic: The Official Government Enquiry*. New York: St. Martin's Press, 1998, p. 26.

At 1:42 p.m. another wireless message concerning reports of ice was received. This message was from the SS *Baltic*, and it too was addressed to the captain of the *Titanic*. It read in part:

> Greek steamer *Athenai* reports passing icebergs
> and large quantities of field ice today in lat.
> 41° 51′ N, long. 49° 52′ W.[5]

Captain Smith also acknowledged receipt of this message.

It would appear that at about 1:45 p.m., on April 14, the following message was sent from the German steamer *Amerika* to the Hydrographic Office in Washington:

> *Amerika* passed two large icebergs in 41° 27′ N,
> 50° 8′ W, on the 14th April.[6]

This message was not intended for the *Titanic*; it was a private one for the hydrographer at Washington. But, as the British enquiry noted, it was passed along to the *Titanic* because she was the nearest to Cape Race, the station to which the message had to be sent in order to reach Washington. It should have been taken to the bridge, since it was a message that affected navigation. However, it seems that it never left the telegraph room; it was certainly not delivered to anyone on the bridge.[7]

At 5:50 p.m., the *Titanic* altered her course from south 62° west to south 86° west true.

---

5   *Report*, p. 26.
6   *Report*, p. 27.
7   *Report*, p. 27.

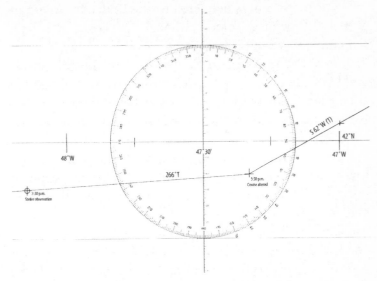

Tracks (paths followed) by *Titanic* to and from
alter-course position, April 14, 1912.

Second Officer Lightoller, who relieved Chief Officer Wilde, came on watch at 6 p.m. He took a six-star observation at 7:30 p.m., 45 minutes after sunset. During the remainder of his watch, the weather was perfectly clear and fine, with not a cloud in the sky. The night was moonless and dark, though, and bitterly cold. The sea was calm.

A message from the SS *Californian* to the SS *Antillian* was picked up by the *Titanic* at 7:30 p.m. It read:

> To Captain, *Antillian*, 6:30 p.m. apparent ship's time; lat. 42° 3′ N, long. 49° 9′ W. Three large bergs five miles to southward of us. Regards.
>
> – Lord.[8]

---

8 *Report*, p. 27.

This message was delivered to the bridge by Assistant Wireless Operator Bride, although he could not later remember to whom it was given.

At 8:55 p.m. Captain Smith came to the bridge. He and Lightoller conversed in general about the night and in particular about the possibility of it being difficult to see ice on such a dark night, considering that there was no wind or swell to make a wash around the base of any iceberg. Smith left the bridge at about 9:20 p.m., saying to Lightoller: "If it becomes at all doubtful let me know at once; I will be just inside."[9] According to Lightoller's later evidence, he interpreted "doubtful" to mean that if there was any doubt at all in his mind about the weather or about the distance at which he could see. He affirmed it was principally those two conditions, but also if the slightest degree of haze were noticeable, then he as well was to notify the captain.[10]

Lightoller took up a position on the bridge at 9:30 p.m. from which he could, in his words, "see distinctly – a view which cleared the back stays and stays and so on – right ahead."[11] He stayed there during the remainder of his watch, keeping as sharp a lookout as possible.

The most crucial message of all was received by the Marconi operators at 9:40 p.m. The message, from a steamer called the *Mesaba*, was in the following terms:

> From *Mesaba* to *Titanic* and all east-bound ships. Ice report in lat. 42° N to 41° 25′ N, long. 49° to long. 50° 30′ W. Saw much heavy

---

9   Transcript of the British enquiry, 13635.
10 British enquiry, 13641.
11 British enquiry, 13676.

pack ice and great number large icebergs. Also field ice. Weather good, clear.[12]

This message clearly indicated the presence of ice across the immediate track of the *Titanic*, about 44 miles ahead. The latitude (41° 25′ N to 42° N) and longitude (49° to 50° 30′ W) coincided with the latitude and longitude at which the *Titanic*, mere hours later, foundered. Yet the message was not delivered to the bridge. As Lightoller stated:

> The one vital report that came through but which never reached the bridge was received at 9:40 p.m. from the *Mesaba*. The position this ship gave was right ahead of us, not many miles distant. The w/o who received it was busy at the time working messages to and from Cape Race, also with his accounts, and he put the message under a paper weight at his elbow, just until he squared up what he was doing, and he would bring it to the bridge *That delay proved fatal and was the main contributory cause to the loss of that magnificent ship and hundreds of lives.*[13]

At 10 p.m. First Officer Murdoch relieved Second Officer Lightoller on the bridge. Lightoller gave Murdoch to understand that the ship was in the ice region and briefed him, in the ordinary course of handing over the ship, on everything he could think of. He passed along Captain Smith's advice to call him immediately if it got at all doubtful and that the captain would be close by.

---

12 *Report*, p. 28.
13 Winocour, p. 281.

Lookouts Fleet and Lee climbed the iron ladder inside the foremast to the crow's nest, relieving lookouts George Symons and Archie Jewell. They received instructions to keep a sharp lookout for small ice and growlers.

Quartermaster Hitchens relieved Quartermaster Olliver at the helm and was given the course north 71° west by compass.

The *Titanic* was steaming towards disaster.

Could the tragedy have been avoided? The accepted premise for mariners of the time – and indeed for mariners before and since – was that in good visibility, ice can be discerned in sufficient time to take evasive action. The *Titanic* had received five wireless reports of field ice and icebergs. Three of them stated there was ice to the north of the *Titanic*'s track; these three messages were delivered to the bridge. Another reported two large icebergs to the south, while the most vital messages of all warned of ice across the *Titanic*'s track. These two messages were never delivered to the bridge. If they had been, it is inconceivable that the ship's speed would not have been reduced and other precautions taken. Nevertheless, given the excellent visibility on the night of April 14, if good seamanship had been practised – by both the bridge and the lookouts – the field ice and icebergs should have posed no threat to the *Titanic*'s safe navigation.

As Captain Arthur Rostron of the rescue ship *Carpathia* noted at the British enquiry, however, one must know what to look for:

> ...people with experience of ice know what to look for, and can at once distinguish that it is a separate object on the water, and it must be only one thing, and that is ice.[14]

---

14   British enquiry, 25437.

Although the bridge crew of the *Titanic* was experienced in North Atlantic crossings, none, including Captain Smith, had had any experience in ice navigation. Lookouts Fleet and Lee were also not experienced in watching out for ice. Apparently they had been told to keep a sharp lookout for small ice and growlers, but on their transatlantic crossings they had never witnessed pack ice or an iceberg, both of which can be easily identified if one knows what to look for.

There have been other marine disasters with a loss of life almost equal to or greater than that of the *Titanic*:

Empress of Ireland	May 30, 1914: loss of 1012 lives
Lusitania	May 7, 1915: loss of 1201 lives
HMS Hood	May 24, 1941: loss of 1415 lives
Bismarck	May 27, 1941: loss of 2090 lives
Wilhelm Gustloff	January 30, 1945: loss of 5348 lives

But none have captured the world's attention in quite the same way.

The *Titanic*, unlike many of the others, did not sink during wartime. Her age was still the age of innocence, of opulence and grandeur. Her tragedy was incomprehensible. Why did the greatest luxury liner of all time not carry enough lifeboats? How could she have collided with an iceberg when most on board felt little or no impact? Why did those entrusted with keeping a safe lookout not recognize the danger ahead until it was too late to take evasive action? What really happened the night she foundered?

The American Senate Investigation, hastily convened under the chairmanship of Senator William Alden Smith just four days after the sinking, accepted testimony from

The *Titanic's* distress message

the survivors and armchair experts at face value. No one on the panel, including Senator Smith, a Midwesterner, was a nautical expert.

The British enquiry, headed by the Right Honourable Lord Mersey, though more formal than the Senate investigation, did not fare any better in its conclusions. To its credit, it did call nautical assessors – Rear Admiral the Honourable S.A. Gough-Calthorpe, CVO, RN and Captain A.W. Clarke; Commander F.C.A. Lyon, RNR – to assist the committee. Neither of these assessors, however, displayed a comprehensive knowledge of ship handling, ice navigation, or hydrodynamic reactions. North Atlantic ship masters were also called as witnesses, but they too gave no real insight into what actually happened on the night of April 14 to 15, 1912.

What follows, I believe, provides the most plausible explanation.

ICEBERG RIGHT AHEAD

The Beginning of the Myth

What did you report when you saw this black mass...?
...I reported an iceberg right ahead.

— *Frederick Fleet to the American inquiry*

The night of April 14, 1912, was moonless, calm, and clear. The water reflected the light from the stars, and there was a lack of definition between the horizon and the sky. One veteran sailor of 26 years said that he had never seen the ocean so flat.

To lookouts Frederick Fleet and Reginald Lee, high in the crow's nest with no shelter to speak of, it was bitterly cold as they faced into the 22-knot wind caused by the ship steaming through the water. The temperature was −15°C with the wind-chill, and dropping.

In fact, the temperature had dropped about 10 degrees since earlier that evening.

The drop in temperature and the warnings of ice in the area had not gone unnoticed by the ship's crew. An order had gone out to ensure that the fresh water supply did not freeze. Sometime between 8:55 p.m. and 9:25 p.m., Second Officer Lightoller and Captain Smith had discussed the possibility that icebergs might be difficult to see on such a clear, calm, moonless night, knowing that because there was no wind or swell, there would be no waves to break up against an iceberg's base. And in the crow's nest, 95 feet above the waterline, Fleet and Lee stood their watch with specific instructions from Lightoller, passed on by Sixth Officer Moody, to "keep a sharp lookout for ice, particularly small ice and growlers."

Fleet and Lee had been on duty since 10 p.m. Their watch was scheduled to finish at midnight. But at 11:30 p.m. they saw, dead ahead and extending to either side, what looked like a shadow on the horizon. They did not bother to report it to the bridge, they later stated, because they believed it to be haze.

The courts of inquiry established there was no haze. The atmospheric conditions precluded any likelihood of it: the weather was perfectly clear, fine, and cold. Second Officer Lightoller himself confirmed that there was no haze during his watch, which lasted until 10 p.m., and that there was no haze when he came to the bridge after the accident.

If Fleet and Lee had known that night what pack ice looked like, they would have recognized it lying three to four miles ahead of the *Titanic*. Instead, and with tragic results, for a full ten minutes the ship steamed towards it at a rate of 22 knots, or 37 feet per second.

At 11:40 p.m., 10 minutes after seeing the "haze," Fleet saw the ice ahead, visibly darker than even the black night and the black sea. At first the object was small, Fleet testified, about the size of two courtroom tables put together, but it became larger and larger with each passing second. He immediately issued the warning by ringing the crow's nest bell three times. Then he reached for the telephone and called the bridge: "Iceberg right ahead!"

Under intense questioning at the inquiries, Fleet and Lee recalled that by the time of impact the height of the ice had increased to approximately 60 feet and extended just above the forecastle head. As Lee described it: "It was a dark mass that came through that haze and there was no white appearing until it was just close alongside the ship, and that was just a fringe at the top."[1]

In daylight, under the ideal weather conditions of April 14, 1912, pack ice would not have been mistaken for an iceberg the height of a forecastle head. But it was precisely those weather conditions that give rise to the optical phenomenon that Fleet and Lee experienced, an optical phenomenon that is well known to ice navigators.

The conditions were ripe for unusual atmospheric distortion. Atmospheric distortion – or abnormal refraction of the atmosphere – occurs whenever there is a strong temperature inversion. On the night of the sinking, there was no wind and there were no clouds, which alone would create a temperature inversion over the surface of the water. The fact that the temperature had dropped considerably since early that evening indicates that the temperature inversion was a very strong one. Since the water was calm and its surface cold because of the proximity of the ice, the abnormal refraction would have occurred just above the waterline. This, in turn, would have produced a distortion in the appearance of objects near the horizon.

Given the absence of the moon that night, the effect would have been magnified by the penetrating rays of the ship's lights. Any object in the path of the lights would

---

1   British enquiry, 2441.

have seemed elevated and would have assumed an exaggerated appearance. Moreover, the object would have loomed from the blackness beyond, startling in its intensity.

The pack ice that the lookouts mistook for haze was probably no more than two metres above the surface of the water. As the ship steamed forward, however, the diffusion of the glow from the masthead light, 145 feet above the waterline and 50 feet above the crow's nest, highlighted the area below and caused the ice in its path to rapidly appear larger and larger. The effect was further intensified at the time of impact, when the light from the ship's many portholes, which were on par with the forecastle head, suddenly "burst" upon the ice field, artificially elevating the ice field to the height of the light itself.

Quartermaster Rowe, stationed on the poop deck, underneath the aft docking bridge, would have experienced a like phenomenon. When the ice passed by him on the starboard side, it appeared to be 100 feet high, no doubt illuminated to that height by the light emanating from the starboard side accommodation portholes. At the British enquiry, Rowe noted that the mass he saw resembling an iceberg passed the *Titanic* only feet away from the stern of the ship; at this time, of course, the rudder was hard to port and the ship was moving ahead at approximately 37 feet per second. Yet, Rowe acknowledged, he heard no scraping of ice along the hull, even though it stood to reason that if the helm had been put hard-a-starboard, the ship's stern would have been up against the berg.[2] That it was not suggests that Rowe's

---

2   It is important to note that in 1912, all helm orders given in ships were applicable to the tiller (See glossary HELM).

100-foot high iceberg, like Fleet and Lee's 60-foot high iceberg, was to some extent a phantom, an illusion of enlargement that faded in the passing light.

At the time of the impact, Fourth Officer Boxhall was just approaching the bridge on the starboard side. By regulation the bridge would have been darkened for

Fourth Officer Joseph G. Boxhall

navigational purposes, so there was no light obstructing his view or otherwise. During his testimony to the inquiries, he stated that when he went to the starboard wing of the bridge, he saw only a black mass very, very low in the water, moving astern of the *Titanic*'s starboard quarter.

Frederick Fleet, photographed after the disaster.

When Fleet sounded the three-bell warning, the ice was about 500 yards ahead. Sixth Officer Moody acknowledged the warning and relayed the message to First Officer Murdoch, who instinctively ordered, "Hard-a-starboard" and "Full speed astern."

Murdoch was in the starboard wing of the bridge when he heard the warning. Since the navigating bridge was forward, approximately 200 feet, or one quarter of the ship's length, abaft the stem, in order to assess the true sense of the ship's heading and rate of turn, he would have had to sight along the centre line or to look aft from the bridge wing, which was 46 feet off the centre line. Objects on one bow, when viewed from the wing of the bridge, may appear to be on the other.

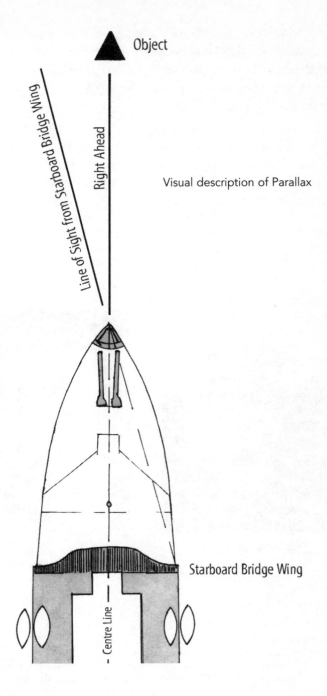

Object

Line of Sight from Starboard Bridge Wing

Right Ahead

Visual description of Parallax

Starboard Bridge Wing

Centre Line

Murdoch undoubtedly saw the object the *Titanic* was heading towards, but because of parallax – the apparent difference in the direction or position of an object when viewed from different points – it would have appeared to him on the starboard bow. His instinctive reaction would have been to turn the ship to port, away from the object. Hence his later remark to Captain Smith, overheard by Boxhall and reported to the American inquiry: "I put her hard-a-starboard and run the engines full astern... I intended to port around it..."[3]

First Officer Murdoch

Quartermaster
Robert Hichens

---

3   Transcript of the American inquiry, p. 230.
    If Murdoch had intended to hard-a-port around it, as stated by Boxhall to the British enquiry, he would not have given the order to reverse the engines.

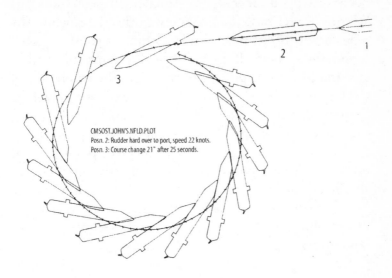

CMSOST.JOHN'S.NFLD.PLOT
Posn. 2: Rudder hard over to port, speed 22 knots.
Posn. 3: Course change 21° after 25 seconds.

Simulator print out

Once Murdoch's orders were given, however, only 37 seconds remained until the time of impact. Quartermaster Hitchens put the helm hard over to starboard. The *Titanic* had veered about two points (22.5 degrees) to port when her starboard bow reportedly struck the iceberg, and then her starboard side "brushed" up against it.

After a vessel, moving at a speed ahead of 37 feet per second, with a hard-to-port rudder that is kept at hard-to-port, has run her starboard bow onto any object, let alone an iceberg, it is physically impossible for that vessel to brush her starboard side along that object. To do so would defy the hydrodynamic reactions of a vessel under way.

A conventional ship steaming ahead steers somewhat similarly to a bus driving in reverse. An appropriate analogy, then, to the *Titanic*'s hydrodynamic reaction at the time of impact is the physical reaction of a bus that has been driving in reverse at 40 kilometres an hour, its steering wheel turned completely to the right, when the left corner of its rear fender strikes against a solid, immoveable object. If the bus's speed is maintained and its steering wheel is kept hard to the right, the whole side of the bus, from the point of impact to the other end, will be destructed. For the side of the bus to simply brush against the object and escape wholesale damage is impossible.

A vessel turns or pivots about its pivot point, a point on its axis whose position and mobility are important to ship handling. The pivot point is not fixed, but when the vessel is steaming through deep water at full speed, the pivot point is about a quarter of the ship's length from the bow (in the vicinity of the bridge area on the *Titanic*). All of this is crucial to note when attempting to swing away from a dangerous object.

Rounding an object "close aboard" requires precise judgment and adaptability. To avoid or to minimize contact damage should an iceberg, for example, be encountered unexpectedly at close quarters, the rudder must be put hard over away from the iceberg. The engine speed must be increased, if not already at full speed ahead. The instant the bow clears or hits the iceberg, the rudder must be put hard over the other way and the engine speed maintained. This is vital in preventing the hull abaft the pivot point from striking the iceberg.

There is no evidence that First Officer Murdoch executed the last manoeuvres, and with only 37 seconds of time, from the giving of the orders until the moment of impact, there would have been no time to carry out his order to go full speed astern. In other words, there was nothing to mitigate the force of the impact.

An iceberg 55 to 60 feet above the water extends 150 to 180 feet below the water – a sheer mass of the hardest glacial ice. If the *Titanic*, travelling at full speed ahead, had hit an iceberg, the force of the impact would have been equal to a momentum of 52,310 tons displacement moving at 37 feet per second. The kinetic energy of the impact would have been enormous. A major part of this energy would have been absorbed almost instantly by the destruction of the ship's hull. The starboard bow contact would have caused a pronounced sheer to port. This, coupled with the thrust of three propellers at full speed ahead against a hard-to-port rudder, would have caused the hull of the ship behind the point of contact to slew and skid heavily to starboard. The resulting interaction between the ship and the iceberg would have caused the whole starboard side of the hull and superstructure to be crushed against the iceberg, while the ship continued to move at full speed ahead. Certainly the hull and possibly the superstructure on the starboard side would have been rent.[4] In all probability, the ship would have flooded, capsized, and sunk within minutes.

Such an impact would have been noticed by all on board. As it was, many passengers slept through the collision and were awakened only by the commotion in the corridors outside their rooms. Those who did notice it almost invariably described it as being of a minor nature.

---

4   From the photographs and videos of the wreck of the *Titanic*, there is no indication of damage to the starboard bow flare and shoulder plates. This area would have been rent had contact been made with an iceberg while the ship was steaming ahead at 37 feet per second against a hard-to-port rudder. It is true that the starboard side railings of the forecastle and well deck are bent inboard, but the port side railings of the forecastle and well deck are also bent or missing. Since the wreck has been submerged in over 2000 fathoms of water for many decades, it is unreliable to attribute the rail damage to ice from an iceberg. Third Officer Pitman, in his evidence to the American inquiry, stated (page 276) that he had gone to the forecastle head to see if there was any damage there but could not see any at all.

Lookout Fleet, in his testimony, said it was "just a slight grinding noise", adding "I thought it was a narrow shave."[5] Fourth Officer Boxhall felt only a "slight impact", not enough to halt him in his walk to the bridge.[6]

Steward Crowe, who was in his cabin on E-deck, 11 feet above the waterline, described it as "a kind of shaking of the ship and a little impact, from which I thought one of the propellers had been broken off."[7] And passenger Elizabeth Shutes said it felt like a "queer quivering [running under her], apparently the whole length of the ship."[8]

In the days following the accident, the media added to the hype surrounding it by publishing photographs of icebergs purporting to be the one that the *Titanic* collided with. One in particular, taken from the deck of the German ship *Prinz Adalbert* on April 15, 1912, showed what appeared to be a strip of red paint along the berg's base. The suggestion that the *Titanic* collided with this iceberg (or any iceberg for that matter) is absurd. Quite simply, paint does not adhere for any length of time to ice. If indeed there was a red discolouration on the surface of that iceberg, most likely it was blood, picked up as a result of the iceberg transitting the seal harvesting area of Newfoundland's east coast, which, a scant month before, had been the scene of the slaughter of hundreds of thousands of seals.

It can only be deduced that before the bridge could take evasive action, the *Titanic* entered a "strip of pack

5   American inquiry, p.321.
6   American inquiry, p. 229.
7   American inquiry, p.614.
8   *Report*, p.v.

ice", which in all probability was infested with multi-year ice and growlers. With her rudder at hard-a-port (hard-a-starboard helm) and the engines at full speed ahead, all of the ice pressure was applied to her starboard bow. This, in turn, caused the piercing of the starboard entrance and shoulder plates, but not the port side plates.[9] As the ship steamed ahead, a channel was made; this channel permitted the hull, abaft number five boiler room, to pass without any holes being made in it.

When it is necessary for a non-ice-strengthened ship to enter pack ice, the entry should be made at the lowest possible speed and on a course that is perpendicular to the ice edge. The ship should never enter the ice at an obtuse angle, since a glancing sideways blow may cause damage to the bow plates and the stern to swing onto the ice. If the ship enters the ice perpendicularly, however, the impact is absorbed by the stem bar and the pressure is evenly distributed to both the port and the starboard entrance, or bow, plates. When entry is made in this manner, even if the speed is unavoidably too high, the chances of damage to the ship are greatly minimized, if not eliminated altogether.

If the *Titanic* had entered the pack ice on a straight course, instead of at the angle dictated by her rudder having been put hard to port, most likely there would have been little or no damage to the ship and in all probability not enough damage to cause her to sink.

---

9   A sonar scan was done in August 1996 on the *Titanic's* starboard bow. The scan revealed six slits of various lengths over a span of less than 100 feet, which meant that the total flooding area was only 12.6 square feet. The scan confirmed the calculations made by Naval Architect Edward Wilding in 1912.

That the *Titanic* entered a strip of pack ice is also not inconsistent with the findings of ice on deck.

Pack ice often has several small pans or pieces of ice – hummocked ice – piled haphazardly on top of it. When a ship's bow makes contact with a floating pan of pack ice, the ice will move away if it is not obstructed by other ice on the outboard side, and a channel will be created that will enable the ship to pass. However, if the floating pan of pack ice is obstructed and cannot move away, either it will break into pieces or its inboard edge will be submerged by the pressure from the ship's bow. If the inboard edge is submerged, the outboard edge will rise and sometimes become vertical, causing the top surface of the floating ice pan to lie flush against the bow plates. Thus, if a ship is moving ahead at a fast rate of speed, some 12 to 15 knots, the impact against the ice will be such that the smaller pieces of ice on top of the floating pan of pack ice will be flipped upwards.

The underwater form of the *Titanic*'s bow was somewhat triangular, with the apex reaching about 33 feet under the surface. When she entered the pack ice, the initial impact would have been with her stem bar and starboard entrance, or bow, plates. Given the speed at which she was travelling, 22 knots, the violence of the impact against obstructed floating pans of ice would easily have resulted in any hummocked ice being flipped at a considerable distance.

It must be remembered that not a lot of ice was found. Fleet told the inquiries he had seen some on the forecastle head and some on the well deck – "not much" – while both Boxhall and Pitman reported finding a little in the well deck. Lightoller saw none at all. Therefore, the reports by a few of those onboard that there was a great deal of ice are simply not credible. If there had been, the lookouts and the officers on deck would have noticed.

In good visibility, pack ice at night is discernible in sufficient time to take evasive action. If Fleet and Lee had informed the bridge that night that they had seen what looked like haze ahead, or if the bridge watch had noticed, almost certainly First Officer Murdoch would have acted. With ten minutes to spare before the ship entered the ice, there would have been ample time to avert the disaster.

The American and British assessors did not comprehend the significance of Fleet and Lee having seen something that looked like haze. Instead, they dismissed it as a fabrication intended to cover up the lookouts' late warning.

Titanic's Final manoeuvre

She never was under a port helm? – She did not come on the port helm, Sir – on the starboard helm.

— Titanic's *QM Robert Hitchens to the British Enquiry*

At both enquiries it was adduced that, at the time of the lookout's warning, *Titanic* was steaming ahead at 22 knots and First Officer Murdoch had ordered the helm hard-a-starboard (rudder hard-a-port) while ordering the engines full astern. It was also adduced that approximately 37 seconds after the lookout's warning, the *Titanic*, having swung two points ($22^{1}/_{2}$ degrees) to port, struck her starboard bow against an iceberg. It was concluded there was no damage abaft number four boiler room. While the experts remain baffled as to why the damage did not extend the whole length of the ship, many have assumed the damage aft was avoided by Murdoch ordering the helm hard-a-port, which turned her back to starboard, after he had turned to port with a hard-a-starboard helm.

To the U.S. Senate inquiry, Fourth Officer Boxhall said he heard First Officer Murdoch tell Captain Smith, *'I put her hard-a-starboard and run the engines full astern, but it was too close; she hit it before I could do any more. I intended to port around it.'*

To the British enquiry he said he heard Murdoch tell Captain Smith: *'I hard-a-starboarded and reversed the engines, and I was going to hard-a-port round it but she was too close. I could not do any more.'*

There is no real evidence to support the contention that Murdoch ordered the *Titanic's* helm hard-a-port. Hydrodynamically, Murdoch's manoeuvre of reversing the engines full speed astern made a turn to starboard impossible with a hard-a-port helm. Therefore, it can only be deduced that he did not in fact order the helm hard-a-port.

Fourth Officer Boxhall, approaching the bridge at the time of impact, heard the three-bell warning, heard Murdoch give the order hard-a-starboard, and heard the engine-room telegraph bells ringing. (Br. Enq. 15346). When he arrived on the bridge a moment later, he noticed the engine room telegraphs showing "FULL SPEED ASTERN" both [engines]. (Br. Enq. 15350). At this point, the cavitation, cause by the propellers turning astern, would have negated all rudder effect. In his evidence to both inquires. Boxhall made no mention of a hard-a-port order. Helmsman Robert Hitchens, in his evidence to both enquiries, categorically denied the hard-a-port order, stating 'She did not come on the port helm, Sir – on the starboard helm.' (Br. Enq. 1316). Hitchens remained at the wheel until 12:23 a.m., 43 minutes after the impact with the ice. Quartermaster Olliver was the only one to give evidence that he heard a hard-a-port order. He stated he was checking the light of the standard compass, situated between numbered two and three funnels, 320 feet abaft the crow's nest, when he heard the three-bell warning. He did not hear the hard-a-starboard order given by Murdoch on the bridge 250 feet away. He said he heard the hard-a-port order after he had arrived on the bridge and 'the iceberg was away up astern.'

When Murdoch ordered the helm hard-a-starboard, the propellers were turning ahead, providing thrust to the rudder; this turned the ship to port two points (22½ degrees) according to Hitchens. By the laws of hydrodynamics, when the *Titanic's* propellers were stopped from turning ahead, the rudder effect decreased; the port turn continued, but the rate of turn decreased. When the propellers were turned astern, all rudder effect was negated due to the cavitation. (It did not matter in which direction or at what angle the rudder was turned, there was no rudder effect.) Momentum continued the turn to port, but the rate decreased to zero when the headway came off the ship.

To turn the *Titanic*, a ship 882 feet in length, back to starboard with a hard-a-port helm (a hard-a-starboard rudder), would require running the engines ahead for a considerable length of time. Boxhall stated '[...] I do not see how it was possible for the *Titanic* to be swinging after the engines were stopped. I forget when it was I noticed the engines were stopped, but I did notice it; and there was absolutely nothing to cause the *Titanic* to swing. (Br. Enq. 15419)'

As a result, there could not have been a starboard turn (hard-a-port helm order) executed to swing the stern away from the illusory iceberg. It can only be deduced that *Titanic* did not collide with an iceberg, but, in fact, transited a 'strip of heavy pack ice,' which in all probability was infested with multi-year ice and growlers.

Under the influence of the surface (Gulf Stream) current *Titanic* remained on a westerly heading until she submerged at 2:20 a.m. It will be remembered that Captain Lord turned the *Californian* to the ENE heading and stopped, after reaching the ice edge. During the remainder of the night, under the influence of the surface (Gulf Stream) current, the *Californian* swung back to a westerly heading, remaining in that direction until gotten under way at 6 a.m.

TESTIMONY ON THE SIGHTING OF ICE

American Inquiry

Subcommittee of the Committee on Commerce
United States Senate New York, N. Y.

Testimony of **Mr Frederick Fleet**

Senator Smith: I want to get on the record the place where you were stationed in the performance of your duty.

Mr Fleet: I was on the lookout.

Senator Smith: In the crow's nest?

Mr Fleet: Yes.

Senator Smith: Did you keep a sharp lookout for ice?

Mr Fleet: Yes, sir.

Senator Smith: Tell what you did?

Mr Fleet: Well, I reported an iceberg right ahead, a black mass.

Senator Smith: When did you report that?

Mr Fleet: Just after seven bells.

Senator Smith: How far away was this black mass when you first saw it?

Mr Fleet: I reported it as soon as ever I seen it.

Senator Smith: What did you report when you saw this black mass Sunday night?

Mr Fleet: I reported an iceberg right ahead.

Senator Smith: How large an object was this when you first saw it?

Mr Fleet: It was not very large when I first saw it.

Senator Smith: How large was it?

Mr Fleet: I have no idea of distances or spaces.

Senator Smith: Was it the size of an ordinary house? Was it as large as this room appears to be?

Mr Fleet: No, no. It did not appear very large at all.

Senator Smith: Was it as large as the table at which I am sitting?

Mr Fleet: It would be as large as those two tables put together, when I saw it at first.

Senator Smith: Did it appear to get larger after you first saw it?

Mr Fleet: Yes, it kept getting larger as we were getting nearer it.

Senator Smith: How large did it get to be, finally when it struck the ship?

Mr Fleet: When we were alongside, it was a little bit higher than the forecastle head.

Senator Smith: The forecastle head is how high above the water line?

Mr Fleet: So that this black mass, when it finally struck the boat, turned out to be about 50 feet above the water?

Senator Smith: Fifty feet, I should say.

Mr Fleet: About 50 or 60.

According to lookout Fleet, when the black mass was first seen at 400 meters away, it looked to be "as large as two tables put together" and kept getting larger as they were getting nearer to it. When it was alongside the starboard bow, he said, it looked to be 50 feet high. What Fleet describes is an illusion of enlargement caused by the ship's lights illuminating the pack ice as the ship sped ahead.

Senator Smith: Do you know whether the ship was stopped after you gave that telephone signal?

Mr Fleet: No, no; she did not stop at all. She did not stop until she passed the iceberg.

Senator Smith: They swung the ship's bow away from the object?

Mr Fleet: Yes, because we were making straight for it.

Senator Smith: But you saw the course altered? And the iceberg struck the ship at what point?

Mr Fleet: On the starboard bow, just before the foremast.

Senator Smith: How far would that be from the bow's end?

Mr Fleet: About 20 feet.

Senator Smith: When she struck this obstacle, or this black mass, was there much of a jar to the ship?

Mr Fleet: No, sir.

Senator Smith: Was there any?

Mr Fleet: Just a slight grinding noise.

Senator Smith: Not sufficient to disturb you in your position in the crow's nest?

Mr Fleet: No, sir.

Senator Smith: Did it alarm you seriously when it struck?

Mr Fleet: No, sir; I thought it was a narrow shave.

Senator Smith: Did any of this ice break onto the decks?

Mr Fleet: Yes, some on the forecastle light and some on the weather deck.

Senator Smith: How much?

Mr Fleet: Not much; only where she rubbed up against it.

Senator Smith: Did Lee and you talk over this black object that you saw?

Mr Fleet: Only up in the nest.

Senator Smith: What did you say about it? What did he say about it to you or what did you say about it to him?

Mr Fleet: Before I reported, I said, "There is ice ahead," and then I put my hand over to the bell and rang it three times, and then I went to the phone.

Senator Smith: What did he say?

Mr Fleet: He said nothing much. He just started looking. He was looking ahead while I was at the phone and he seen the ship go to port.

Senator Smith: Who sighted the black mass first; you or Lee?

Mr Fleet: I did. I say I did, but I think he was just as soon as me.

Testimony of Mr George Thomas Rowe

Senator Burton: Where were you the night of the collision?

Mr Rowe: I felt a slight jar and looked at my watch. It was a fine night, and it was then 20 minutes to 12. I looked toward the starboard side of the ship and saw a mass of ice. I then remained on the after bridge to await orders through the telephone. No orders came down, and I remained until 25 minutes after 12, when I saw a boat on the starboard beam.

Senator Burton: Did you see any ice when on the watch?

Mr Rowe: No, sir; only when we struck, when we passed it on the starboard side.

Senator Burton: About how high was that iceberg?

Mr Rowe: Roughly, 100 feet, sir.

Senator Burton: Was there anything distinctive about the color of that iceberg?

Mr Rowe: No a bit, sir; just like ordinary ice.

Senator Burton: You saw it as it was brushing by?

Mr Rowe: Yes, sir. It was very close to the ship, almost touching it.

Senator Burton: Was the helm over when you passed the iceberg?

Mr Rowe: That I could not say.

Senator Burton: Just where were you when you saw the iceberg?

Mr Rowe: On the poop, sir; underneath the after bridge.

Senator Burton: You were located practically right on the stern of the boat?

Mr Rowe: Right on the stern, sir; the poop.

Senator Burton: And the iceberg, when the boat rubbed against it, was right near, was it?

Mr Rowe:	Yes, sir.
Senator Burton:	How far, would you say?
Mr Rowe:	It was so near that I thought it was going to strike the bridge.
Senator Burton:	Did it strike the bridge?
Mr Rowe:	No, sir; never.
Senator Burton:	Only 10 or 20 feet away?
Mr Rowe:	Not that far, sir.
Senator Burton:	Did you notice the iceberg when the boat got clear of it?
Mr Rowe:	No, sir. I went on the bridge then, to stand by the telephone.
Senator Burton:	Could you hear the ice scraping along on the boat where you were?
Mr Rowe:	No, sir.
Senator Burton:	So you do not know whether it was rubbing against the hull there or not?
Mr Rowe:	No, sir.
Senator Burton:	What is your best judgment about that?
Mr Rowe:	I do not think it was.
Senator Burton:	You are positive you heard no rubbing?
Mr Rowe:	Yes, sir.
Senator Burton:	Do you not think that if the helm

had been hard-a-starboard the stern would have been up against the berg?

Mr Rowe: It stands to reason it would, sir, if the helm were hard-a-starboard.

Senator Burton: Were you able to form any judgment as to how long that berg was?

Mr Rowe: No, sir.

Senator Burton: How near were you to the starboard side of the boat when you first noticed it rubbing?

Mr Rowe: About 8 or 10 feet. I went to the side.

Senator Burton: Did you go immediately to the side?

Mr Rowe: Yes, sir.

Senator Burton: Were you reading the log that night?

Mr Rowe: As soon as the berg was gone I looked at the log and it read 260 miles. The log was reset at noon. I had charge of the taffrail log, which was a Neptune log.

Senator Burton: You read the log each hour, did you not?

Mr Rowe: Every two hours. I read it at 10 o'clock, but I do not remember what it was, now, sir.

Senator Burton: Do you remember what speed she was making, or did you make any computation?

Mr Rowe:	No, sir. We read the log every two hours, and it is telephoned to the bridge and entered in the quartermaster's log book. It is taken from there every watch and put into the ship's log.
Senator Burton:	How long did the rubbing or grinding against the ice last?
Mr Rowe:	I never heard anything except the first contact; the first jar was all I knew about it. I never heard any rubbing at all.
Senator Burton:	Do you think the propeller hit the ice? Did you feel any jolt like the propeller hitting the ice?
Mr Rowe:	No, sir.
Senator Burton:	Do you not think the propeller would have hit the ice if the helm had been turned hard-a-starboard?
Mr Rowe:	Yes, sir.

Testimony of Mr Robert Hitchens

Senator Smith:	What is your business?
Mr Hitchens:	Quartermaster.
Senator Smith:	What was your post of duty; where was it?
Mr Hitchens:	At the time of the collision I was at the wheel, sir, steering the ship.

Senator Smith: How long had you been at the wheel
when the collision occurred?

Mr Hitchens: One hour and forty minutes, sir.

Senator Smith: I wish you would tell now, in your own
way, what occurred that night from the
time you went on watch until the
collision occurred.

Mr Hitchens: I went on watch at 8 o'clock... At
10 o'clock I went to the wheel, sir.
Mr Murdoch come up to relieve
Mr Lightoller. I had the course given
me from the other quartermaster, north
71° west, which I repeated to him, and
he went and reported it to the first
officer or the second officer in charge,
which he repeated back – the course,
sir. All went along very well until 20
minutes to 12, when three gongs came
from the lookout, and immediately
afterwards a report on the telephone,
"Iceberg right ahead." The chief officer
rushed from the wing to the bridge, or I
imagine so, sir. Certainly I am inclosed
in the wheelhouse, and I can not see,
only my compass. He rushed to the
engines. I heard the telegraph bell ring;
also give the order, "Hard-a-starboard,"
with the sixth officer standing by me to
see the duty carried out and the
quartermaster standing by my left side.
Repeated the order, "Hard-a-starboard.
The helm is hard over, sir."

Senator Smith: Who gave the first order?

Mr Hitchens: Mr Murdoch, the first officer, sir; the
officer in charge. The sixth officer
repeated the order, "The helm is hard-a-
starboard, sir." But, during the time, she
was crushing the ice, or we could hear
the grinding noise along the ship's
bottom. I heard the telegraph ring, sir.
The skipper came rushing out of his
room – Capt. Smith – and asked, "What
is that?" Mr Murdoch said, "An
iceberg." He said, "Close the emergency
doors."

Testimony of Mr Joseph Groves Boxhall

Senator Smith: What is your vocation?

Mr Boxhall: Mariner.

Senator Smith: Where were you when the collision
took place?

Mr Boxhall: I was just approaching the bridge.

Senator Smith: On the port or the starboard side?

Mr Boxhall: Starboard side.

Senator Smith: Did the collision occur on the port or
the starboard side?

Mr Boxhall: On the starboard side, sir.

Senator Smith: And you were on deck at that time?

Mr Boxhall: On the deck, sir.

Senator Smith: Approaching the bridge.

Mr Boxhall: Just approaching the bridge.

Senator Smith: Could you see what had occurred?

Mr Boxhall: No, sir; I could not see what had occurred.

Senator Smith: Did you know what had occurred?

Mr Boxhall: No, not at all. I heard the sixth officer say what it was.

Senator Smith: What did he say that it was?

Mr Boxhall: He said we had struck an iceberg.

Senator Smith: Was there any evidence of ice on any of the decks, to your knowledge, after that collision?

Mr Boxhall: Just a little on the lower deck. On the open deck I saw just a little, not much.

Senator Smith: Did you continue to go toward the bridge after the impact?

Mr Boxhall: Yes, sir.

Senator Smith: How far did you go?

Mr Boxhall: At the time of the impact I was just coming along the deck and almost abreast of the captain's quarters, and I heard the report of three bells.

Senator Smith: What kind of a report? Describe it.

Mr Boxhall: The lookout's report.

Senator Smith: What was said?

Mr Boxhall: Three bells were struck.

Senator Smith: Three bells?

Mr Boxhall: That signifies something has been seen ahead. Almost at the same time I heard the first officer give the order "Hard-a-starboard," and the engine telegraph rang.

Senator Smith: What did the order mean?

Mr Boxhall: Ordering the ship's head to port.

Senator Smith: Did you see this iceberg at that time?

Mr Boxhall: Not at that time.

Senator Smith: Did it extend above the deck that you were on?

Mr Boxhall: Oh, no, sir, it did not extend there.

Senator Smith: Do you know whether it struck the bow squarely?

Mr Boxhall: It seemed to me to strike the bluff of the bow.

Senator Smith: Describe that.

Mr Boxhall: It is in the forward part of the ship, but almost on the side.

Senator Smith: On which side?

Mr Boxhall: It is just where the ship begins to widen out on the starboard side.

Senator Smith: But it was not a square blow on the bow of the ship?

Mr Boxhall: No, sir.

Senator Smith: In ordinary parlance, would it be a glancing blow?

Mr Boxhall: A glancing blow.

Senator Smith: Was the blow felt immediately?

Mr Boxhall: A slight impact.

Senator Smith: How slight?

Mr Boxhall: It did not seem to me to be very serious. I did not take it seriously.

Senator Smith: Slight enough to stop you in your walk to the bridge?

Mr Boxhall: Oh, no, no, no.

Senator Smith: Heavy enough to stop you, I mean?

Mr Boxhall: No, sir.

Senator Smith: So slight that you did not regard it as serious?

Mr Boxhall: I did not think it was serious.

Senator Smith: Did you proceed to the bridge?

Mr Boxhall: Yes, sir.

Senator Smith: Whom did you find there?

Mr Boxhall: I found the sixth officer and the first officer and captain.

Senator Smith: The sixth officer, the first officer and the captain?

Mr Boxhall: Yes, sir.

Senator Smith: All on the bridge together?

Mr Boxhall: Yes, sir.

Senator Smith: What, if anything, was said by the captain?

Mr Boxhall: Yes, sir. The captain said, "What have we struck?" Mr Murdoch, the first officer, said, "We have struck an iceberg."

Senator Smith: Then what was said?

Mr Boxhall: He followed on to say – Mr Murdoch followed on to say, "I put her hard-a-starboard and run the engines full astern, but it was too close; she hit it."

Senator Smith: That was before she struck?

Mr Boxhall: No, after.

Senator Smith: That was after she struck?

Mr Boxhall: Yes.

Senator Smith: He said that he put her hard-a-starboard?

Mr Boxhall: Yes, sir.

Senator Smith: But it was too late?

Mr Boxhall: Yes, sir.

Senator Smith: And she hit it?

Mr Boxhall: Yes, sir.

Senator Smith: What did the captain say?

Mr Boxhall: Mr Murdoch also said, "I intended to port around it."

Senator Smith: "I intended to port around it?"

Mr Boxhall: "But she hit before I could do any
                     more."

Senator Smith: What else did he say?

Mr Boxhall: We all walked out to the corner of the
                     bridge then to look at the iceberg.

Senator Smith: The captain?

Mr Boxhall: The captain, first officer, and myself.

Senator Smith: Did you see it?

Mr Boxhall: I was not very sure of seeing it. It
                     seemed to me to be just a small black
                     mass, not rising very high out of the
                     water, just a little on the starboard
                     quarter.

Senator Smith: How far out of the water should you
                     judge?

Mr Boxhall: I could not judge the size of it, but it
                     seemed to me to be very, very low lying.

Senator Smith: Did it extend up to B-deck?

Mr Boxhall: Oh, no; the ship was past it then. It
                     looked to me to be very, very low in the
                     water.

At the same time Quartermaster Rowe, who was on the poop deck looking forward along the starboard side, where the port hole lighting shone to the height of the boat deck, witnessed an illusion of enlargement – low-lying ice appearing to be an iceberg extending 100 feet high.

Senator William Smith,
Michigan.

Senator
Furnifold M. Simmons,
North Carolina.

Senator
Theodore E. Burton, Ohio.

Senator
Duncan U. Fletcher, Florida.

Senator George C. Perkins,
California.

Senator
Jonathan Bourne Jr.,
Oregon.

Senator
Francis G. Newlands,
Nevada.

TESTIMONY ON THE SIGHTING OF ICE
British Inquiry

Wreck Commissioners' Court

Scottish Hall, Buckingham Gate, 1912

Proceedings on a Formal Investigation ordered by the
Board of Trade into the loss of the *S.S. Titanic*

Frederick Fleet, *Sworn.*
Examined by the Attorney-General.

17245   Now at the time you went into the crow's nest, which would be at 10 o'clock on that night, was the sky clear? – Yes.

17246   The sea we know was very calm? – The sea calm.

17247   The stars shining? – Yes.

17248   Could you clearly see the horizon? – The first part of the watch we could.

17249   The first part of the watch you could? – Yes.

17250   After the first part of the watch what was the change if any? – A sort of slight haze.

17251   A slight haze? – Yes.

17252   Was the haze on the water line? – Yes.

17253   It prevented you from seeing the horizon clearly? – It was nothing to talk about.

17254   It was nothing much, apparently? – No.

17255   Was this haze ahead of you? – Yes.

17256   Was it only ahead, did you notice? – Well, it was only about two points on each side.

17257   When you saw this haze did it continue right up to the time of your striking the berg? – Yes.

17258   Can you give us any idea how long it was before you struck the berg that you noticed the haze? – No, I could not.

17259   Can you tell us about how long you had been on duty before you noticed the haze? – I could not say. I had no watch.

17260   I want you to give us some idea. You came on duty at 10 o'clock. We know that the berg was struck at about 11:40. That gives us an hour and 40 minutes, during which time you were in the crow's nest all the time. That is right, is it not? – Yes.

You say the first part of the watch it was clear and then there came this change which you have described. I want you to give some idea of when it was you noticed the change – when it got to a haze.

17261   (*The Witness*) Well, I daresay it was somewhere near seven bells.

The haze-like phenomenon was noticed at "somewhere near seven bells", which would have been at 11:30 p.m. The impact with the ice occurred at 11:40 p.m. Therefore, the lookouts noticed the "haze" ten minutes before the impact with the ice, when the ice was approximately three to four miles away.

17262   (*The Attorney-General*) Somewhere near seven bells, which would be half past 11? – Yes.

17263   Did you say anything to your mate about it? – Well, I told him there was a slight haze coming.

17264   Is that Lee? – Lee.

17265   All the time that you noticed the haze was there anything in sight? – No.

17266   Did it interfere with your sight ahead of you? – No.

17267   Could you see as well ahead and as far ahead after you noticed the haze as you could before? – It did not affect us, the haze.

17268   It did not affect you? – No, we could see just as well.

17269   You did not report it then, I gather from that? – No.

17270   You did not say anything about it to the bridge? – No.

(*The Commissioner*) I mean the evidence before and after the accident is that the sky was perfectly clear, and therefore if the evidence of the haze is to be accepted, it must have been some extraordinary natural phenomenon – something that sprang up quite suddenly, and then vanished.

(*The Attorney-General*) Yes.

The atmospheric conditions the night the ship sank precluded any likelihood of haze: the weather was perfectly clear, fine, and cold. It would be unusual for haze to be so narrowly defined as to be 45° wide (extending two points on each side) and to have so little depth that the ship could steam through it in a matter of seconds. What Fleet refers to, however, does indicate a strip of pack ice that was about three miles long and a quarter of a mile wide.

17273   (*The Commissioner – To the Witness*) I understand you to say that whatever it was, it made no difference to the look-out? – Yes, my Lord.

17274   (*The Attorney-General*) Who was it first saw the berg? Was it you or Lee? – Well, I do not know.

17275   Well, which of you gave the signal? – I did. You were looking ahead. Will you tell my Lord what it was – what you saw? (*The Commissioner*) This is the three bell signal.

17276   (*The Attorney-General*) Yes, we are coming to it, the three bell signal, something ahead. (*To the Witness*) Now describe to my Lord what it was you saw? – Well, a black object.

17277   A black object. Was it high above the water or low? – High above the water.

17278   What did you do? – I struck three bells.

17279   Was it right ahead of you, or on the port or
        starboard bow? – Right ahead.

17280   You struck three bells immediately, I suppose?
        – Yes, as soon as I saw it.

17281   What did you do next? – I went to the
        telephone.

17282   Was that on the starboard side of the crow's
        nest? – Yes.

17283   You went to the telephone, and – ? – Rang them
        up on the bridge.

17284   Did you get an answer? – Yes.

17285   Did you say anything to them at once, or did
        they answer you before you told them? – I asked
        then were they there, and they said yes.

17286   Yes? – Then they said, "What do you see?" I
        said, "Iceberg right ahead." They said, "Thank
        you."

17287   Then you dropped the telephone, did you? – Yes.

17288   What did you do next? – I kept the lookout
        again.

17289   You were approaching the berg meanwhile? –
        Yes.

17290   Are you able to give us the distance, or about
        the distance, the berg was from your ship when
        you first saw it? – No.

17291   And except for what happened you have
        nothing to guide you as to the time either, have
        you? – No.

17292   We must get it from the events. Did you notice any change in the heading of your vessel after you gave this report? – After I rang them up on the phone and looked over the nest she was going to port.

17293   You were looking over the nest. Were you still on the starboard side of the nest? – No; my place is on the port, but I went to starboard to telephone.

17294   Did you remain there when you dropped the telephone, or did you go back to your own place? – I went back to my own place again.

17295   It would be on the port side of the crow's nest? – On the port side.

17296   You saw her head turn to port, I think I understood you to say? – Yes. Was the vessel still turning to port when she struck the berg, can you tell us?

17297   (*The Commissioner*) Do not say you can if you cannot? – She went to port all right, and the berg hit her on the starboard bow.

17298   (*The Attorney-General*) She went to port. Do you mean she had a slight turn to port? – Well, going to port.

17299   She was still going to port when the berg struck her? – On the starboard bow.

17300   When you saw the vessel strike you felt it, did you; could you see it? – Certainly.

17301   What did you see when that happenend? Your vessel, as I understand you, was going to port.

Then you say she struck an iceberg. Tell us what you saw. You were in the crow's nest, watching it, were you not? – Yes.

17302   Did you see any ice come on the deck? – Yes, some on the forecastle head and some on the well deck.

17303   Could you tell how high, at all, the berg was? – No, I could not.

17304   You could not tell us in feet, of course, or measurement in that way, but can you give us any idea; was it as high as you were? – Just a little bit higher than the forecastle head.

(*The Commissioner*) It may have been standing about 75 feet above the surface of the water.

17312   (*The Attorney-General*) Yes, that is probably as near as we should ever get to it. (*To the Witness*) You say the berg passed, did you? – Yes.

17313   As you were looking over to the starboard side of the ship? – Yes.

17314   Could you give us some idea of what it looked like when it came. Was it a great big mass that passed you, or was it a small mass that you could see? – Well, a great big mass.

17315   Do you mean like a great block? – Yes.

17316   When you saw it first could you form an idea what height it was? – No.

17317   Well, it looked smaller, presumably? – Yes.

When the "berg" was first seen at 400 metres away it looked to be low in the water, yet seconds later, when it was alongside the starboard bow, it looked to be 50 feet high. What Fleet witnessed is an optical phenomenon that is well known to ice navigators.

17318   Then did you remain on the crow's nest? – Yes.

17319   Until eight bells? – Till eight bells went.

Robert Hitchens, *Sworn.*
Examined by the Attorney-General.

893   Are you a quartermaster? – Yes.

895   Do you remember the Sunday, the day of the collision with an iceberg? – Yes.

945   Do you remember the vessel striking? – Yes.

946   Did you notice the time when she struck? – Yes.

947   What was it? – Twenty minutes to twelve.

948   Had you any instructions before she struck? Had you been told to do anything with your helm before she struck? – Just after she struck I had the order, "Hard-a-starboard" when she struck.

949   Just as she struck is that what you said? – Not immediately as she struck; the ship was swinging. We had the order, "Hard-a-starboard," and she just swung about two points when she struck.

950   You got the order, "Hard-a-starboard"? – Yes.

951   Had you time to get the helm hard-a-starboard before she struck? – No, she was crashing then.

952   Did you begin to get the helm over? – Yes, the helm was barely over when she struck. The ship had swung about two points.

953   She had swung two points? – Yes.

954   (*The Commissioner*) Do let me understand; had she swung two points before the crash came? – Yes, my Lord.

955   (*The Attorney-General*) I am not quite sure I understand what you had done to the helm before this. You had got an order, "Hard-a-starboard"? – "Hard-a-starboard," yes.

956   You proceeded at once to put the wheel hard-a-starboard? – Immediately, yes.

957   Before the vessel struck had you had time to get the wheel right over? – The wheel was over then, hard over.

958   (*The Commissioner*) Before she struck? – Oh yes, hard over before she struck.

       (*The Attorney-General*) I rather understood him to say the opposite before. I do not think he understood.

       (*The Commissioner*) Let me see if I understand it. Someone gave an order, " Hard-a-starboard."

       (*The Attorney-General*) Yes.

       (*The Commissioner*) This was before she struck?

       (*The Attorney-General*) Yes.

       (*The Commissioner*) He put the wheel hard over?

       (*The Attorney-General*) Yes, and got it hard over.

(*The Commissioner*) And got it hard over. The ship moved two points?

(*The Attorney-General*) That is right.

(*The Commissioner*) She did not move any more, because, as I understand, the crash came?

959   (*The Attorney-General*) Exactly, that is the story.

(*To the Witness*) Who gave the order, "Hard-a-starboard?" – Mr Murdoch, the First Officer.

961   Did the Fourth and Sixth Officers, Mr Boxhall and Mr Moody, remain? – Mr Moody was standing behind me when the order was given.

962   And was Mr Boxhall on the bridge? – From what I am given to understand, Mr Boxhall was approaching the bridge.

963   Was Captain Smith on the bridge? – No, Sir.

964   Do you know where he was? – Yes, Sir; in his room.

965   So far as you know, was there any change in the speed at which the vessel was travelling before she struck? – I took the log which was part of my duty at half a minute to ten, as near as I can tell, and the vessel was going 45 knots by the Cherub log every two hours.

966   Forty-five knots? – Forty-five was registering on the log.

967   (*The Commissioner*) Was the speed altered before the collision? – Well, the crash came immediately.

968   I know it did. Had the speed been altered
       before? – No, I could not say, my Lord, because I
       could not see the officer on the bridge. I am in
       the wheel house. I cannot see anything only my
       compass.

969   (*The Attorney-General*) I think we can get at it
       in this way. What was the first notice to you
       that there was something ahead? – Three gongs
       from the crow's nest, Sir.

970   That you would hear in the wheelhouse, would
       you? – Certainly.

971   And you knew what that meant? – Certainly, Sir.

972   That meant something ahead? – Yes.

973   How long was that before the order came,
       "Hard-a-starboard?" – Tell, as near as I can tell
       you, about half a minute.

974   In order that we may understand, if there was a
       telephone message from the crow's nest to the
       bridge, would you hear it? Would you know
       anything about it? – Certainly so, Sir.

975   Would you indicate on the model where you
       were, where the wheelhouse is? – Yes. (*The
       Witness indicated the position on the model.*)

975a   (*The Commissioner*) And the crow's nest is just
       on the mast in the front, is it not? – Just above
       the eyes of the fore-rigging.

976   (*The Attorney-General*) Put your finger on it?
       – Yes. (*The Witness did so.*)

977   I think that is the indication of it, is it not?
       – Yes.

978   Then there is the telephone. What was the
        telephone message? Did you hear any? – I did
        not hear the message, but I heard the reply.

979   What was the reply? – "Thank you."

980   Who gave it? – Mr Moody.

981   Then it means this, that Mr Moody, the Sixth
        Officer, got a telephone message after the three
        bells had been struck? – Immediately after.

982   You did not hear what was said to Mr Moody,
        but you heard him acknowledge the message,
        and say, "Thank you?" – Yes, I heard Mr Moody
        repeat, "Iceberg right ahead."

983   To whom did he repeat that? – To Mr Murdoch,
        the First Officer.

984   "Iceberg right ahead," is that what he said?
        – Yes.

985   Repeating what he had heard from the
        telephone message? – Yes.

986   And then what happened? – I heard Mr
        Murdoch rush to the telegraph and give the
        order, "Hard-a-starboard."

987   When you say he rushed to the telegraph, is that
        the telegraph to the engine room you are
        speaking of? – Yes.

988   The order, "Hard-a-starboard" was to you? – Yes.

        (*The Commisioner*) What order did he give to
        the engine room?

989   (*The Attorney-General*) I do not think he knows.
        (*To the Witness*) Do you know what order it was

that was telegraphed down to the engine room?
– No.

990   I think your Lordship will hear that it was,
"Stop: full speed astern." – Now just for a
minute give me your attention on the point of
speed. You have told us according to the log
that the speed was 45 knots in two hours? – Yes.

991   Up to the time of hearing the three bells struck,
was there any change of speed at which the
vessel was proceeding? – No, none whatever.

992   And the order, if any, that was given with regard
to the speed would be the order by telegraph to
the engine room, which you have told us you do
not know? – I do not quite understand you.

993   You have just told us what happened: first of all,
the signal of the three bells, then the telephone
message, then it was repeated to the First
Officer, "Iceberg right ahead"; then the First
Officer went to the telegraph to give an order to
the engine-room and gave you the order, "Hard-
a-starboard?" – Yes.

994   At any rate up to his going to the telegraph
as I follow you, there was no change of speed?
– No, Sir.

995   What that order was you do not know? –
No, Sir.

996   Then "Hard-a-starboard," and you immediately
put up your helm? – Hard-a-starboard.

997   Right over? – Yes.

998   What is it, 35 degrees? – 40 degrees.

999   Then you got the helm right over? – Right over, Sir.

1000   Then she comes round two points and then strikes. Is that right? – The vessel veered off two points; she went to the southward of west.

1001   And then she struck? – Yes.

1004   And no lights were in the wheelhouse at all except the compass light? – And the small light.

1005   And the small light on the course board? – Yes.

      (*The Commissioner*) The report from the crow's nest was "Iceberg ahead."

1006   (*The Attorney-General*) "Iceberg right ahead." (*To the Witness*) The helm was put hard-a-starboard? – Yes.

1007   And the ship moved two points? – Yes.

1008   Assuming the iceberg was right ahead, I should like to see what difference the two points would make, and what part of the ship would then be presented to the iceberg? – Yes.

1009   (*The Attorney-General*) It is a mere question of taking the indication of course. (*To the Witness*) Did any one of the officers see you carry out the order? – Yes.

1010   Who? – Mr Moody, and also the Quartermaster on my left. He was told to take the time of the collision.

1011   Let us get the fact of what happened. Was Mr Moody there when you put the helm hard-a-starboard? – That was his place, to see the duty carried out.

1012   Was it his duty to report it? – Yes, he reported the helm hard-a-starboard.

1013   To whom? – To Mr Murdoch, the First Officer.

1014   Then you had put the helm hard-a-starboard and Mr Moody had reported hard-a-starboard to Mr Murdoch? – Yes.

1014   (*The Attorney-General*) That is the only fact your Lordship had not got in the story.

(*The Commissioner*) I do not see the significance of it.

1015   (*The Attorney-General*) It is only because you cannot fix the time except by seeing exactly what happened. That is the point of it. The estimate of time is of very little value, but if you can get what happened you can form an estimate. So that he had reported, and then it was after that that she strikes, is that right? – She struck almost at the same time.

1016   Almost as he reported it? – Yes.

1017   How long did you remain at the wheel? – Until 23 minutes past 12.

1019   After she struck, did you notice at all what happened? – No.

1020   Did you notice whether the ship had stopped? – Oh, yes, the ship had stopped.

1021   Can you tell us how long it was after the
         collision that you noticed that the ship had
         stopped? – Immediately.

1023   You remained at your post? – Yes.

1024   I suppose you heard some of what was going on?
         – I heard a few words of command, that was all.

1025   Tell us what you heard in the way of command?
         – Just about a minute I suppose, after the
         collision, the Captain rushed out of his room
         and asked Mr Murdoch what was that, and he
         said, "An iceberg, Sir," and he said, "Close the
         watertight door."

         (*The Commissioner*) Wait a minute. A minute
         after the collision, Captain Smith –

1026   (*The Attorney-General*) Came out of his room on
         to the bridge do you mean? – Yes, Sir, he passed
         through the wheelhouse on to the bridge.

1027   He rushed out of his room through the
         wheelhouse on to the bridge? – Yes.

1028   And asked Murdoch, "What is that?" – Yes.

1029   And Murdoch said, "An iceberg." Is that right?
         – Yes.

1030   Mr Murdoch said "An iceberg," and then? – The
         Captain immediately gave him orders to close
         the watertight doors. He said, "They are already
         closed." He immediately then sent for the
         carpenter to sound the ship.

1032   Could you see them being closed? – I could not see anything but my compass.

1033   Where you were you would not be able to see it? – No.

1045   When the vessel struck did you feel any shock? – Yes, I felt the ship tremble, and I felt rather a grinding nature along the ship's bottom.

1046   While you were in the wheelhouse you had the compass in front of you? – Yes.

1047   Could you see at all ahead through the wheelhouse? – I could not see anything.

1048   You would not be able to see the iceberg even if it had been quite clear. Is that what you mean? – No, I could not see it, on no account whatever could I see it.

1049   You said that the Captain rushed out of his room through the wheelhouse to the bridge? – Yes.

1050   Where was his room? I do not know if you can point it out on the model. Was it on the starboard or port side? – The starboard side.

Examined by Mr Holmes

1314   You were given the order to hard-a-starboard? – Yes.

1315   Was that the only order you had as to the helm? – Yes.

(*Mr Holmes*) Because, if your Lordship will remember, the evidence of the witness Scarrott on Friday was quite the contrary, when he came up on deck.

(*The Commissioner*) What did he say?

(*Mr Holmes*) He said that the ship appeared to be under a port helm, and appeared to be going around the iceberg towards the starboard side.

(*The Commissioner*) Did he say so?

(*The Attorney-General*) Yes, I think so.

1316   (*Mr Holmes*) It is Question 354. (*To the Witness*) She never was under a port helm? – She did not come on the port helm, Sir – on the starboard helm.

Although witness Scarrott and others may have contradicted Quartermaster Hitchens in this aspect of his testimony, it is Hitchens's word that has the air of credibility. It is inconceivable that Hitchens, steering the ship under such circumstances, would not know the helm order he was executing at that time. Nevertheless, once the engines were turning astern, regardless of how the rudder was turned, cavitation nullified the rudder effect.

Joseph Groves Boxhall, *Sworn.*
Examined by Mr Raymond Asquith.

13505   Were you the Fourth Officer of the *Titanic* at the time of this accident? – I was.

13506   What certificate do you hold? – Extra master.

13507   You have held that, I think, for about four or five years? – September, 1907.

15342   Was the first intimation that there was ice about the striking of the three bells, so far as you were concerned? – No, when we struck the berg; that was the first.

15343   Do you mean you felt the shock before you heard the bells? – No, I heard the bells first.

15344   Where were you at that time? – Just coming out of the Officers' quarters.

15345   How soon after you heard the bells did you feel the shock? – Only a moment or two after that.

15346   Did you hear an order given by the First Officer? – I heard the First Officer give the order, "Hard-a-starboard," and I heard the engine room telegraph bells ringing.

15347   Was that before you felt this shock, or afterwards? – Just a moment before.

15348   (*The Commissioner*) Let us be clear about that. The order, "Hard-a-starboard," came between the sound of the bells and the collision? – The impact, yes.

15349   (*Mr Raymond Asquith*) Did you go on to the bridge immediately after the impact? – I was almost on the bridge when she struck.

15350   Did you notice what the telegraphs indicated with regard to the engines? – "Full speed astern," both.

15351   Was that immediately after the impact? – Yes.

15352   Did you see anything done with regard to the watertight doors? – I saw Mr Murdoch closing them then, pulling the lever.

15353   And did the Captain then come out on to the bridge? – The Captain was alongside of me when I turned round.

15354   Did you hear him say something to the First Officer? – Yes, he asked him what we had struck.

15355   What conversation took place between them? – The First Officer said, "An iceberg, Sir. I hard-a-starboarded and reversed the engines, and I was going to hard-a-port round it but she was too close. I could not do any more. I have closed the watertight doors." The Commander asked him if he had rung the warning bell, and he said, "Yes."

Because of cavitation, it is hydrodynamically impossible to hard-a-port around an object once the engines have been reversed.

15356   Did the Captain and the First Officer go to the starboard side of the bridge to see if they could see the iceberg? – Yes.

15357   Did you see it yourself? – I was not too sure of seeing it. I had just come out of the light, and my eyes were not accustomed to the darkness.

15366   When you got to C-deck did you see some ice there on the deck? – Yes, I took a piece of ice out of a man's hand, a small piece about as large as a small basin, I suppose, very small, anyhow, about that size (*describing*). He was going down again to the passenger accommodation, and I took it from him and walked across the deck to see where he got it. I found just a little ice in the well deck covering a space of about three or four feet from the bulwarks right along the well deck, small stuff.

Lord Mersey, Wreck Commissioner

Commander F.C. Lyon

Rear-Admiral S.A. Gough-Calthorpe

Professor J. Harvard Biles

Edward C. Chaston

Captain A.W. Clarke

Attorney-General Sir Rufus Issacs, KC

PASSENGERS' TESTIMONY ON THE SIGHTING OF ICE

Subcommittee of the Committee on Commerce
United States Senate New York, N. Y.

Testimony of Mr J. Bruce Ismay
Mr J. Bruce Ismay, being duly sworn by the chairman,
testified as follows:

Senator Smith: Mr Ismay, for the purpose of simplifying this hearing, I will ask you a few preliminary questions. First state your full name, please?

Mr Ismay: Joseph Bruce Ismay.

Senator Smith: And your place of residence?

Mr Ismay: Liverpool.

Senator Smith: And your age?

Mr Ismay: I shall be 50 on the 12th of December.

Senator Smith: And your occupation?

Mr Ismay: Ship owner.

Senator Smith:	Are you an officer of the White Star Line?
Mr Ismay:	I am.
Senator Smith:	In what capacity?
Mr Ismay:	Managing Director.
Senator Smith:	Were you a voluntary passenger?
Mr Ismay:	A voluntary passenger, yes.
Senator Smith:	Will you describe what you did after the impact or collision?
Mr Ismay:	I presume the impact awakened me. I lay in bed for a moment or two afterwards, not realizing, probably, what had happened. Eventually I got up and walked along the passageway and met one of the stewards, and said, "What has happened?" He said, "I do not know, sir."
	I then went back into my room, put my coat on, and went up on the bridge, where I found Capt. Smith. I asked him what had happened, and he said, "We have struck ice." I said, "Do you think the ship is seriously damaged?" He said, "I am afraid she is." I then went down below, I think it was, where I met Mr Bell, the chief engineer, who was in the main companionway. I asked if he thought the ship was seriously damaged, and he said he thought she was, but was quite satisfied the pumps would keep her afloat.

I think I went back onto the bridge. I heard the order given to get the boats out. I walked along to the starboard side of the ship, where I met one of the officers. I told him to get the boats out...

Testimony of Maj. Arthur G. Peuchen
The witness was sworn by the chairman.

Senator Smith: Will you kindly give the reporter your full name?

Maj. Peuchen: Arthur Godfrey Peuchen.

Senator Smith: Were you aboard the vessel *Titanic* when it sailed from Southampton?

Maj. Peuchen: I was.

Senator Smith: Where were you located on the vessel? Where were your quarters and where were your friends located?

Maj. Peuchen: I was located on C-deck, stateroom 104, and they were located on A-deck, I think A 2. I forget Mr Allison's number, but most of my friends were on A-deck.

Senator Smith: The upper deck?

Maj. Peuchen: Just below the bridge, I should think; just below the upper deck. I guess you are right, sir.

Senator Smith: Well, I want it in the record, Major.

Maj. Peuchen: Sunday evening I dined with my

friends,... We sat chatting and
smoking there until probably
20 minutes after 11, or it may have
been a little later than that. I then bid
them good night and went to my room.
I probably stopped, going down, but I
had only reached my room and was
starting to undress when I felt as
though a heavy wave had struck our
ship. She quivered under it somewhat.
If there had been a sea running I would
simply have thought it was an unusual
wave which had struck the boat; but
knowing that it was a calm night and
that it was an unusual thing to occur
on a calm night, I immediately put my
overcoat on and went up on deck. As I
started to go through the grand stairway
I met a friend, who said, "Why, we
have struck an iceberg." He said, "If
you will go up on the upper deck" or "If
you will go up on A-deck, you will see
the ice on the fore part of the ship." So
I did so. I went up there. I suppose the
ice had fallen inside the rail, probably
4 to 4½ feet. It looked like shell ice,
soft ice. But you could see it quite
plainly along the bow of the boat...
He said, "No matter what we have
struck, she is good for 8 or 10 hours".

Testimony of Mr C.E. Henry Stengel

Senator Smith: What is your full name?

Mr Stengel: C.E. Henry Stengel.

Senator Smith: Where do you reside?

Mr Stengel: Newark, N. J.

Senator Smith: What is your business?

Mr Stengel: Leather manufacturer.

Senator Smith: Were you a passenger on board the *Titanic* on the ill-fated voyage from Southampton to the place of the accident?

Mr Stengel: Yes, sir.

Senator Smith: Where were you when the accident happened?

Mr Stengel: I had retired. My wife called me. I was moaning in my sleep. My wife called me, and says, "Wake up; you are dreaming," and I was dreaming; and as I woke up I heard a slight crash. I paid no attention to it until I heard the engines stop. When the engines stopped I said, "There is something serious; there is something wrong. We had better go up on deck." I just put on what clothes I could grab, and my wife put on her kimono, and we went up to the top deck and walked around there. There were not many people around there.

Testimony of Mr Archibald Gracie
The witness was sworn by the chairman.

Senator Smith: Give us your full name and address.

Mr Gracie: Archibald Gracie, 1527 Sixteenth Street NW, Washington, D.C.

Senator Smith: And your business?

Mr Gracie: Historian.

Senator Smith: Colonel, you were one of the passengers on the ill-fated *Titanic*. Will you kindly, as succinctly and as tersely as possible, in your own way, trace the principal events leading up to the sinking of that ship on Sunday night, April 14?

Mr Gracie: Do you want me to tell everything of my own knowledge, specifying in each case where it is outside of my own knowledge?

Senator Smith: We are particularly anxious for such information as bears upon the completeness of the ship, upon her management as you observed it, upon her equipment so far as you are able to testify to it, and the conduct of her officers and crew.

Mr Gracie: I was awakened in my stateroom at 12 o'clock. The time, 12 o'clock, was noted on my watch, which was on my dresser, which I looked at promptly when I got up. At the same time, almost instantly, I heard the blowing off of steam, and the ship's machinery seemed to stop.

It was so slight I could not be positive of it. All through the voyage the machinery did not manifest itself at all from my position in my stateroom, so perfect was the boat. I looked out of the door of my stateroom, glanced up and down the passageway to see if there was any commotion, and I did not see anybody nor hear anybody moving at all; but I did not like the sound of it, so I thought I would partially dress myself, which I did, and went on deck.

I went on what they call the A-deck. Presently some passengers gathered around. We looked over the sides of the ship to see whether there was any indication of what had caused this noise. I soon learned from friends around that an iceberg had struck us.

Presently along came a gentleman, described by Mr Stengel here, who had ice in his hands. Some of this ice was handed to us with the statement that we had better take this home for souvenirs...

Colonel Gracie did not feel any impact. Like Maj. Peuchen, his stateroom was on C-deck. He was awakened in his stateroom at 12 o'clock, 20 minutes after the impact. As he was getting up, he heard steam blowing off, at which time the ship's machinery seemed to stop. The impact was so slight he could not be positive of it.

Testimony of Mrs J. Stuart White

Testimony taken separately before Senator William Alden Smith, chairman of the subcommittee.

The witness was sworn by Senator Smith.

Senator Smith: Do you make the Waldorf-Astoria your permanent home, Mrs White?

Mrs White: My home really is Briarcliffe Lodge; Briarcliffe Manor, N. Y. That is my summer house. When I am in New York, I am always here at the Waldorf-Astoria.

Senator Smith: I want to ask one or two questions, Mrs White, and let you answer them in your own way. You were a passenger on the *Titanic*?

Mrs White: Yes.

Senator Smith: Where were your apartments on the *Titanic*? What deck were you on?

Mrs White: We were on deck C.

Senator Smith: Were you aroused especially by the impact?

Mrs White: No; not at all. I was just sitting on the bed, just ready to turn the lights out. It did not seem to me that there was any very great impact at all. It was just as though we went over about a thousand marbles. There was nothing terrifying about it at all.

Senator Smith: Were you aroused by any one of the ship's officers or crew?

Mrs White: No.

Senator Smith: Do you know whether there was any alarm turned in for the passengers?

Mrs White: We heard no alarm whatever. We went immediately on deck ourselves.

Senator Smith: You went on deck?

Mrs White: We went right up on deck ourselves.

Senator Smith: On the upper deck?

Testimony of Mrs Helen W. Bishop
The witness was sworn by the chairman.

Senator Smith: What is your full name?

Mrs Bishop: Mrs Helen W. Bishop.

Senator Smith: You were on board the *Titanic* on this ill-fated voyage?

Mrs Bishop: Yes.

Senator Smith: Did anything in particular occur to attract your attention to the ship or any special feature of the ship while you were en route from Southampton to the place of this accident?

Mrs Bishop: We thought of nothing at all except the luxury of the ship; how wonderful it was.

Senator Smith: I wish you would tell the committee what you did after learning of this accident.

Mrs Bishop: My husband awakened me at about a quarter of 12 and told me that the boat had struck something. We both dressed and went up on the deck, looked around, and could find nothing. We noticed the intense cold; in fact, we had noticed that about 11 o'clock that night. It was uncomfortably cold in the lounge. We looked all over the deck; walked up and down a couple of times, and one of the stewards met us and laughed at us. He said, "You go back downstairs. There is nothing to be afraid of. We have only struck a little piece of ice and passed it." So we returned to our stateroom and retired. About 15 minutes later we were awakened by a man who had a stateroom near us. We were on B-deck, No. 47. He told us to come upstairs. So we dressed again thoroughly and looked over all our belongings in our room and went upstairs.

Testimony of **Daniel Buckley**

Testimony taken separately before Senator William
Alden Smith, chairman of the subcommitee.

The witness was sworn by Senator Smith.

Senator Smith: Mr Buckley, where do you live?

Mr Buckley: 855 Trent Avenue, Bronx.

Senator Smith: Where did you get aboard the *Titanic*?

Mr Buckley: At Queenstown.

Senator Smith: How did you happen to come over to
America?

Mr Buckley: I wanted to come over here to make
some money. I came in the *Titanic*
because she was a new steamer. This
night of the wreck I was sleeping in my
room on the *Titanic*, in the steerage.
There were three other boys from the
same place sleeping in the same room
with me.

I heard some terrible noise and I
jumped out on the floor, and the first
thing I knew my feet were getting wet;
the water was just coming in slightly.
I told the other fellows to get up, that
there was something wrong and that
the water was coming in. They only
laughed at me. One of them says:
"Get back into bed. You are not in
Ireland now."

Before the completion of the *Titanic* a number of artist's impressions were made of the ship for publicity purposes

1. An artist's impression of the promenade deck on TITANIC.

2. An artist's impression of the second-class promenade deck on TITANIC.

3. An artist's impression of a second-class stateroom on TITANIC.

4. An artist's impression of an en-suite bathroom on TITANIC.

5. An artist's impression of the elevator terminus on TITANIC.

6. Confirmation of Father Browne's ticket on TITANIC, Father Browne's photographs would document its maiden voyage.

7. Advertising poster for TITANIC.

8. A postcard advertising the White Star Line, owners of TITANIC.

9. Raising the anchor, taken by Father Browne.

Before the completion of the *Titanic* a number of artist's impressions were made of the ship for publicity purposes

1. An artist's impression of the promenade deck on TITANIC.

2. An artist's impression of the second-class promenade deck on TITANIC.

3. An artist's impression of a second-class stateroom on TITANIC.

4. An artist's impression of an en-suite bathroom on TITANIC.

5. An artist's impression of the elevator terminus on TITANIC.

6. Confirmation of Father Browne's ticket on TITANIC, Father Browne's photographs would document its maiden voyage.

7. Advertising poster for TITANIC.

8. A postcard advertising the White Star Line, owners of TITANIC.

9. Raising the anchor, taken by Father Browne.

I got on my clothes as quick as I could, and the three other fellows got out. The room was very small, so I got out, to give them room to dress themselves. Two sailors came along, and they were shouting: "All up on deck! unless you want to get drowned."

When I heard this, I went for the deck as quick as I could. When I got up on the deck I saw everyone having those life belts on only myself; so I got sorry, and said I would go back again where I was sleeping and get one of those life preservers; because there was one there for each person.

I went back again, and just as I was going down the last flight of stairs the water was up four steps, and dashing up. I did not go back into the room, because I could not. When I went back toward the room the water was coming up three steps up the stairs, or four.

Testimony of Olaus Abelseth

Testimony taken separately before Senator William Alden Smith, chairman of the subcommitee.

The witness was sworn by Senator Smith.

Senator Smith: How old are you?

Mr Abelseth: 26 years of age in June.

Senator Smith: Did you sail on the *Titanic?*

Mr Abelseth: Yes.

Senator Smith: I wish you would tell the reporter when you first knew of this collision, and what you did, and where you were in the ship. I believe you were a steerage passenger?

Mr Abelseth: Yes, sir.

Senator Smith: In the forward part of the ship?

Mr Abelseth: Yes. I was in compartment G on the ship.

Senator Smith: Go ahead and tell us just what happened.

Mr Abelseth: I went to bed about 10 o'clock Sunday night, and I think it was about 15 minutes to 12 when I woke up; and there was another man in the same room – two of us in the same room – and he said to me, "What is that?" I said, "I don't know, but we had better get up." So we did get up and put our clothes on, and we two went up on deck in the forward part of the ship.

Then there was quite a lot of ice on the starboard part of the ship. They wanted us to go down again, and I saw one of the officers, and I said to him: "Is there any danger?" He said, "No." I was not satisfied with that, however, so I went down and told my brother-in-law and my cousin, who were in the same compartment there. They were not in the same room, but they were just a little ways from where I was. I told them about what was happening, and I said they had better get up. Both of them got up and dressed, and we took our overcoats and put them on. We did not take any life belts with us. There was no water on the deck at that time.

Testimony of George A. Harder
Testimony taken separately before Senator William Alden Smith, chairman of the subcommitee.

The witness was sworn by Senator Smith.

Senator Smith: State your name and place of residence, please.

Mr Harder: George A. Harder; 117 Eighth Avenue, Brooklyn.

Senator Smith: Were you a passenger aboard the *Titanic*?

Mr Harder: I was.

Senator Smith: What stateroom did you have?

Mr Harder: We had E-50; that is on E-deck.

Senator Smith: What occurred Sunday night between the hours of 11 and 12 o'clock?

Mr Harder: About a quarter to 11 I went down to my stateroom with Mrs Harder and retired for the night; and at 20 minutes to 12 we were not asleep yet, and I heard this thump. It was not a loud thump; just a dull thump. Then I could feel the boat quiver and could feel a sort of rumbling, scraping noise along the side of the boat.

When I went to the porthole I saw this iceberg go by. The porthole was closed. The iceberg was, I should say, about 50 to 100 feet away. I should say it was about as high as the top deck of the boat. I just got a glimpse of it, and it is hard to tell how high it was.

Senator Smith: What did you do then?

Mr Harder: I thought we would go up on deck to see what had happened; what damage had been done. So we dressed fully and went up on deck, and there we saw quite a number of people talking; and nobody seemed to think anything serious had happened. There were such remarks as "Oh, it will only be a few hours before we will be on the way again."

It is impossible to see any object in the darkness outside, through the glass of a porthole, from inside a lighted room. The appearance of an iceberg 50 to 100 feet away, was either an optical illusion or an exaggeration.

Testimony of Mr Berk Pickard
Before Senator William Alden Smith, at the
Waldorf-Astoria Hotel.

The witness was sworn by Senator Smith.

Senator Smith: State your name, age, residence, and
occupation.

Mr Pickard: Berk Pickard; No. 229, Hebrew
Immigrant Society. At the time I took
passage on the *Titanic* I came from
London. I am thirty-two years old. I am
a leather worker; a bag maker. I was
born in Russia, in Warsaw. My name
was Berk Trembisky. I was for a long
time in France and I assumed a French
name. As regards private business, I am
Pickard.

I was one of the third-class passengers
on the *Titanic*. My cabin was No. 10 in
the steerage, at the stern. I first knew of
the collision when it happened, about
10 minutes to 12. We had all been
asleep, and all of a sudden we perceived
a shock. We did not hear such a very
terrible shock, but we knew something
was wrong, and we jumped out of bed
and we dressed ourselves and went
out...

Testimony of **Mr Norman Campbell Chambers**
Testimony taken separately before Senator William
Alden Smith, chairman of the subcommittee.

The witness was sworn by Senator Smith.

Senator Smith: Please state your full name, and
residence.

Mr Chambers: Norman Campbell Chambers,
111 Broadway, New York.

Senator Smith: What is your business?

Mr Chambers: Mechanical Engineer.

Senator Smith: You were on board the *Titanic* on this
ill-fated voyage?

Mr Chambers: Yes, sir.

Senator Smith: I wish you would tell the committee
what you know about the collision, and
any circumstances leading up to or
subsequent to the impact, which may
tend to throw light upon this
unfortunate affair.

First, did you, after the impact, observe
the condition of the watertight
compartments?

Mr Chambers: Our stateroom was E-8, on the
starboard side; that is the lowest berth
deck, and as far as I know, we were as
far forward as any of the first-cabin
passengers on that deck.

At the time of the collision I was in bed, and I noticed no very great shock, the loudest noise by far being that of jangling chains whipping along the side of the ship. This passed so quickly that I assumed something had gone wrong with the engines on the starboard side.

Senator Smith: What did you do then?

Mr Chambers: At the request of my wife I prepared to investigate what had happened, leaving her dressing. I threw on sufficient clothes, including my overcoat. I went up, in a leisurely manner, as far as the A-deck on the starboard side. There I noted only an unusual coldness of the air. Looking over the side I was unable to see anything in any direction.

Senator Smith: I desire printed in the record also an affidavit received by me made by Mrs E.B. Ryerson, of Chicago, Ill.

The affidavit referred to is as follows:

State of New York,
County of Otsego, as:

Emily Borie Ryerson, being duly sworn, deposes and says, I reside in the city of Chicago, Ill. I was a passenger on the steamship *Titanic* on April 14, 1912. At the time of collision I was awake and heard the engines stop, but felt no jar. My husband was asleep, so I rang and asked the steward, Bishop, what was the matter. He said, "There is talk of an iceberg, ma'am, and they have stopped, not to run into it." I told him to keep me informed if there were any orders. It was bitterly cold, so I put on a warm wrapper and looked out the window (we were in the large cabins on the B-deck, very far aft) and saw the stars shining and a calm sea, but heard no noise. It was 12 o'clock. After about 10 minutes I went out in the corridor, and saw far off people hurrying on deck. A passenger ran by and called out, "Put on your life belts and come up on the boat deck"...

Senator Smith: I offer also to be printed in the record, an affidavit made by Daisy Minahan, [...]

The affidavit [...] referred to is as follows:

State of Wisconsin,
Wood County, as:

Daisy Minahan, being first duly sworn, upon oath deposes and says: I was asleep in stateroom C 78; the crying of a woman in the passageway awakened me. I roused my brother and his wife, and we began at once to dress. No one came to give us warning. We spent five minutes in dressing and went on deck to the port side...

Yours,
Daisy Minahan

Senator Smith: I submit, to be printed in the record, the following affidavit of James R. McGough:

I, James R. McGough, do depose and say that I was a passenger on the steamship *Titanic* on Sunday, April 14, 1912, the time of the disaster; that I live in Philadelphia, Pa.; that I am thirty-six years of age; and I hereby make the following statement:

I was awakened at 11:40 p.m., ship time; my stateroom was on the starboard side, deck E, and was shared with me by Mr Flynn, a buyer for Gimbel Bros., New York, at Thirty-third and Broadway. Soon after leaving our stateroom we came in contact with the second dining room steward, Mr Dodd, in the companionway, of whom we asked the question, "Is there any danger?" and he answered, "Not in the least," and suggested that we go back to bed, which we did not, however, do.

Senator Smith: I submit also the statement of Mrs Lucian P. Smith, to be printed in the record.

Statement of Mrs Lucian P. Smith,
One of the survivors of the Titanic

At 7:30 p.m., as usual, my husband and I went to dinner in the café..... I stayed up until 10:30, and then went to bed.

..... I was asleep when the crash came. It did not awaken me enough to frighten me; in fact, I went back to sleep again. Then I awakened again, because it seemed that the boat had stopped. About that time my husband come into the room. Still I was not frightened, but thought he had come in to go to bed. I asked him why the boat had stopped, and, in a leisurely manner, he said, "We are in the north and have struck an iceberg: It does not amount to anything, but probably delay us a day getting into New York. However, as a matter of form, the captain has ordered all ladies on deck."

THE BRIDGE AND THE CROW'S NEST

Is it possible that the man in the crow's nest would have a better opportunity than you had [on the bridge] of observing whether or not there was a haze? – No.

You say you would have as good as an opportunity where you were stationed on the bridge? – Better.

— Second Officer Lightoller to the British Enquiry

Lookouts, Fleet and Lee came under close examination at the inquiries. Time and again they were relentlessly questioned about their role in the tragedy, so much so that at least Fleet, feeling under the gun, at one point rebelliously broke out and asked the examiners: "Is there any more likes to have a go at me?"[1]

There can be no doubt that if Fleet and Lee had reported the first sighting of the "haze" to the bridge, First Officer Murdoch would have had time to avoid the accident. To hold the lookouts responsible for the sinking, however, would be unjust. Incredible as it seems, it was not the duty of the men in the crow's nest to report any sighting of haze to the bridge. Their duty was to report a physical object that was ahead and to either side. They

---

1   British enquiry, 17479

would not have had the experience or the expertise to identify anything out of the ordinary, especially something like pack ice at night.

All too often it was the practice of the bridge to rely on the crow's nest lookout to report the sighting of anything ahead or to either side. Yet the advantage of maintaining a lookout from the crow's nest instead of from the bridge is minimal. Generally speaking, everything visible from the crow's nest is equally visible, if not even more so, from the bridge. As Arthur Rostron, captain of the *Carpathia*, colourfully pointed out in answer to the question of whether there was any point in putting men in the crow's nest if things could be picked up first from the bridge:

> It does not necessarily say we shall pick them up quicker from the bridge, but naturally an officer is more on the *qui vive*; he is keener on his work than a man would be, and he knows what to look for. He is more intelligent than a sailor.[2]

Intelligence aside, it is difficult to see how any sailor who was standing in an open iron cage almost a hundred feet above the water, facing into the biting wind, could be keen on his work. At best, his eyes would have been stinging from the cold while he stood in misery for a two-hour watch. At worst, his ability to concentrate would have been so severely affected by the cold as to render his watch useless. Those conditions were not conducive to keeping an effective lookout. In this regard, at least, the officers on the bridge had a definite advantage.

---

2   British enquiry, 25445

In the *Titanic's* case, the bridge was just 70 feet abaft the crow's nest. the distance to the sea horizon from the crow's nest was $11^3/_4$ miles; from the bridge, nine and a half – a difference of only two and a quarter miles. The difference was negligible. In the opinion of Second Officer Lightoller at least, those stationed on the bridge were in fact in a better position than those in the crow's nest to detect anything unusual ahead.[3]

Although Lightoller was quick not to blame First Officer Murdoch's bridge watch for not having kept an effective lookout, he implied to the British enquiry that if ice had been encountered during his watch, the tragedy in all likelihood would have been avoided. According to his testimony, at about 9:30 p.m., when the ship was approaching the longitude at which ice was expected, he took up a position on the bridge that would enable him to see directly ahead. He said that he remained in that position for the rest of his watch and, with the aid of binoculars, kept a sharp lookout for ice and an eye in general on the weather and prevailing conditions. Because of these "extra precautions," he confidently told the enquiry, he would have seen the ice in "sufficient time to clear it – quite sufficient."[4]

Fleet and Lee saw the haze-like phenomenon at 11:30 p.m., without the aid of binoculars, because there were no binoculars in the crow's nest. At that time, Murdoch was stationed on the bridge, with binoculars at hand. At the time of the sighting, the ice was three to four miles distant, ten minutes away. There was plenty of time to take evasive action, yet the *Titanic* continued on its course at 22 knots.

---

3   British enquiry, 25445
4   British enquiry, 14340

Starboard side view of the *Titanic* depicting the crow's nest and the starboard bridge wing shelter.

If Murdoch had kept a lookout similar to the one Lightoller kept, he would have seen, at 11:30 p.m. or even earlier, the pack ice that Fleet and Lee mistook for haze. As an experienced officer he would have known that anything sighted ahead was a warning to navigate with caution. If he had seen the phenomenon the lookouts later described, by the authority vested in him as the senior watch officer, he would have taken evasive action immediately.

Why the bridge watch did not notice the ice before the lookouts' warning will never be known. Two of the officers on the bridge – Murdoch and Moody – did not survive the sinking; those who did offered no testimony about any extenuating circumstances that would have precluded an effective lookout. Certainly resources were not an issue. Murdoch's watch consisted of three highly certified deck officers – Murdoch himself, Boxhall, and Moody – all of whom were master mariners. There were also three quartermasters – Hitchens, Rowe, and Olliver – in addition to the two lookouts in the crow's nest. A total of eight deck watch personnel, six of them on deck, were charged with the responsibility of keeping a safe watch as the ship neared what were reported to be ice-infested waters.

Yet, according to Boxhall's testimony before the British enquiry, Murdoch was the only officer on the bridge to keep a lookout during that particular watch.[5] Boxhall stated that although he, himself, was on watch, he was not on the bridge, nor was he on lookout duty. He testified that from 8 p.m. on, he was computing stellar observations and that he was emerging from the officers' quarters when the three-bell warning was struck.[6] From the other testimony at the enquiry, it was revealed that when the ship entered the ice, Moody was standing next to Hitchens in the wheelhouse, Rowe was standing watch at the stern of the ship, and Olliver was on standby duty and checking the standard compass, which was positioned between funnels numbered two and three about 250 feet abaft the bridge.

It is useless to speculate about what Murdoch was doing that prevented him from seeing the ice until it was too late. Whatever insight he could have provided was lost when he was lost with the ship. Nevertheless, it does seem clear that he overly relied on the lookouts in keeping the watch. He was not the first bridge watch officer to have done so, nor was he likely the last, but in this case it was an unfortunate error in judgment that had resounding consequences.

---

5   British enquiry, 15564
6   British enquiry, 15337 and 15344

IN DEFENCE OF CAPTAIN SMITH

Captain Smith... was doing only that which other skilled
men would have done in the same situation.

— *Right Honourable Lord Mersey,*
Wreck Commissioner

History has been especially unkind to Captain Smith.
Charges of recklessness have dogged his reputation and
much of the blame for the tragedy has been laid squarely
at his feet.

In reality, he was an accomplished seaman. During his
more than 40 years at sea, he had spent 25 as a ship's
commander in the White Star Line. Although it can be
argued his record was not impeccable, before the tragedy
little fault was found with it. Certainly he had earned the
esteem of both his crew and his employers. In the words of
Second Officer Charles Lightoller, "Captain 'E.J.' was one
of the ablest skippers on the Atlantic."[1]

But once the initial shock over the sinking had
subsided, allegations of attempting a record crossing and
speeding while ignoring warnings of ice in the area were
levelled at Captain Smith. These allegations were
groundless, for several reasons:

---

1   Winocour, p.282

In the first instance, because of the coal strike that England was facing, the *Titanic* had sailed without full bunkers. As K.C. Barnaby points out in *Some Ship Disasters and their Causes*, "this alone would have prevented any attempt at a record crossing."[2]

It is also inconceivable that Chief Engineer Joseph Bell would have permitted the engines to be fully opened up on what was in fact a maiden voyage. Although the captain of a ship is, generally speaking, the supreme commander of that ship, it is the chief engineer who is *de facto* commander in the engine room. Except in cases of emergency, it is the chief engineer, and not the captain, who makes the final decision on the vessel's rate of speed.

Second, it is obvious from the evidence that Captain Smith did not ignore warnings of ice in the area. To the contrary, he made every effort to avoid the ice of which he was aware.

To begin with, as the British report noted, the very route the *Titanic* took was designed to avoid "as much as possible the areas where fog and ice are prevalent at certain seasons, without thereby unduly lengthening the passage across the Atlantic."[3] The route, known as the "Outward Southern Track," followed the arc of a great circle between Fastnet Light, on the southwest coast of Ireland, and a point in latitude 42° N and longitude 47° W (often called the "turning point"). Once the turning point was reached, the route (more commonly referred to as the "customary track" from then on) went by Rhumb Lines to the Nantucket Shoal light vessel, off the east coast of the United States, and then on to New York. Up until the time of the disaster, this route was the accepted route for out-bound mail steamers going from Fastnet Light to

2   Barnaby, p. 104
3   *Report*, p. 24

Nantucket Shoal light vessel. The usual ice limits lay some 25 miles north of the Outward Southern Track.

As Second Officer Lightoller recalled in later years, however, ice conditions in the spring of 1912 were unusual. "Under normal conditions," he said, "we should have proved to be well south of the usual ice limits; only in this case the ice limit had moved very many miles south, due solely to the immense amount of ice released in the Arctic."[4] Much of the ice that made its way that year into the Gulf Stream area, and from there into the shipping lanes of the North Atlantic, was composed of extremely hard multi-year ice and growlers. Ice of this type is quite capable of piercing a ship's hull and is extremely hazardous to shipping if due diligence and caution are not exercised.

Nevertheless, despite the shifting ice limits, Captain Smith was undoubtedly aware as he approached the coast of Newfoundland that he was approaching an area in which ice and bergs could be sighted. This does not necessarily mean ice was expected, but rather, in the words of Second Officer Lightoller, "that there was the possibility of seeing ice, as there always is when crossing the Banks."[5]

That there was ice in the area was confirmed by a message the *Titanic* received, at 9 a.m. on April 14, from the *S.S. Coronia*. This message, which Captain Smith acknowledged, referred to bergs, growlers, and field ice, sighted two days before, on April 12, in 42° N from 49° to 51° W. Since the ice referred to was eight miles north of the *Titanic*'s customary track to New York, it was not necessary for Captain Smith, on the strength of this message, to take any avoiding action.

---

4   Winocour, p.281
5   Winocour, p.281

A second message, this time from the S.S. *Baltic*, was more crucial. The *Baltic*'s message, received at 1:42 p.m. and also acknowledged by Captain Smith, fixed icebergs and large quantities of field ice in latitude 41° 51′ N, longitude 49° 52′ W. A computation placed this ice 129 miles, 266° true, from the "turning point" of 42° N, 47° W, or two miles north of what would be the *Titanic*'s customary track of south 85° west (265°) true. The *Titanic* was expected to reach this turning point at 5 p.m. In the ordinary course of events, her captain would then have ordered the ship's course altered to the customary track. Captain Smith, however, was aware that ice lay only two miles north of this route and that avoiding action, to take him further south of the ice field, was called for. As the evidence from the subsequent inquiries suggests, he took this action in ordering that his course of south 62° west (242°) true be held for 50 minutes beyond the turning point and not be altered to south 86° west (266°) true until 5:50 p.m. It was a sound course of action. When, at 11 p.m., the *Titanic* passed the ice reported in the *Baltic*'s message, she did so without incident.

A third message regarding ice in the area was intercepted by the *Titanic* at 7:30 p.m. This message, originally from the captain of the *Californian* to the captain of the *Antillian*, reported icebergs at 41° 58′ N, 49° 09′ W. It would appear that the message was delivered to the bridge, although it could not later be ascertained to whom it was given. In any event, the ice along this route, like that reported earlier in the day by the S.S. *Coronia*, was about eight miles north of the *Titanic*'s track and no cause for concern.

At 7:30 p.m. Second Officer Lightoller and Fourth Officer Boxhall obtained an accurate fix from a six-star sight. This position fix placed the *Titanic*'s track four miles south of all reported ice, safe enough by any standards.

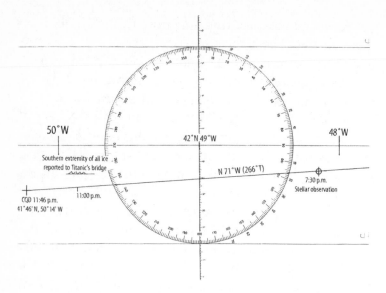

Track (path followed) four miles south of all ice reported
to *Titanic's* bridge.

It is clear that Captain Smith did act appropriately on
the information he was given about the ice along the
Titanic's track. The most crucial message of all, however,
was never delivered to the bridge. This was the message
from the *S.S. Mesaba*, reporting ice in latitude 42° N. to
41° 25′ N., longitude 49° to 50° 30′ W – right within the
Titanic's track.

Third, although it cannot be denied that the *Titanic*
was travelling at some 21½ to 22 knots when she entered
the ice-infested waters, maintaining full speed in good
visibility until ice was actually sighted was – and remains
– the practice of the day. At the British court of enquiry,
no fewer than 15 North Atlantic Ocean masters testified
that even when ice conditions were present, if visibility
was good they continued at full speed until they were
within sight of the ice field. And, by his own admission,
Captain A.H. Rostron, on the rescue ship *Carpathia*, also

ran his ship at full speed to and through the ice-infested waters that had been the scene of the sinking a few hours before. He, too, relied on the premise that ice would be sighted, as it was, in time to take evasive action.[6]

Nevertheless, even though Captain Smith was not aware that ice lay across his path and had no reason to reduce his speed until ice was actually sighted, the allegation that he was reckless was blatantly made at the British enquiry. As Mr Thomas Scanlan, M.P., said, during his questioning of Second Officer Lightoller:

> What I want to suggest to you is that it was recklessness, utter recklessness, in view of the conditions which you have described as abnormal, and in view of the knowledge you had from various sources that ice was in your immediate vicinity, to proceed at $21\frac{1}{2}$ knots?[7]

Lightoller's answer, however, was quick in its defence: "Then all I can say," he replied, "is that recklessness applies to practically every commander and every ship crossing the Atlantic Ocean."[8] It was, he insisted, "normal navigation, which embodies careful navigation" and was not indicative in the least that those in charge of the vessel were negligent in any way.[9]

---

6   Granted, the captain of the *Carpathia* also testified at the 1912 Senate investigation that before speeding into ice-infested waters, he had doubled his lookouts, taken extra precautions, and exerted extra vigilance. It must be remembered, however, that he knew he was entering a dangerous zone, which had just been the scene of a serious accident. It should also be noted that when he was queried at the investigation on what would be a safe, reasonable speed for a vessel the size of the *Titanic*, on the course the *Titanic* was taking, and in the proximity of icebergs, he neatly sidestepped the question by stating that he knew absolutely nothing about the ship. (American inquiry, p. 27)

7   British enquiry, 14414

8   British enquiry, 14414

9   British enquiry, 14416 and 14425

In the final analysis, Captain Smith was exonerated by the Lord Mersey, chairman of the British enquiry. In his report to the British Parliament, Lord Mersey stated:

> I am not able to blame Captain Smith.[. . .] he was doing only that which other skilled men would have done in the same situation.[10]

Second Officer Lightoller, in his memoirs, was more explicit in dismissing the allegation that Captain Smith was accountable for the tragedy:

> . . . accusations of recklessness, carelessness, not taking precautions, or driving his ship at too high a speed, were absolutely and utterly unfounded; but the armchair complaint is a common disease, and generally accepted as one of the necessary evils from which the seafarer is condemned to suffer.[11]

Regardless of what actions could have been taken and should have been taken, there will always be those, with vision behind them, willing to presume what they would have done under like conditions. Many an armchair judge has stated, in retrospect, what Captain Smith should have done on the night of April 14, 1912. But what he did do was simply what every other master has done: he maintained the speed of his vessel, knowing that if ice was sighted, he would have time to take evasive action. The tragic difference was that the *Titanic*'s bridge watch did not notice the pack ice until it was too late to evade it, while the lookouts mistook it for haze and didn't bother to report it.

---

10 *Report*, p. 30
11 Winocour, p.282

THE BOARD OF TRADE REGULATIONS

...as a result of what has happened with regard to the Titanic, *it is clear there should be a larger number of boats provided.*

— *The Attorney-General*

When tragedy strikes, we seek to lay blame. It makes us less vulnerable somehow, less susceptible to the vagaries of nature, to point the finger and pronounce that if proper care had been taken, the event would never have happened.

Today, as we enter a new millennium, we are astounded at the 1912 British Board of Trade regulations – regulations that were meant for ships measuring up to 10,000 gross tons but were equally acceptable for ships that were the size of the *Titanic*.

Titanic was a 46,329 gross ton, state-of-the-art, twentieth-century ship. She carried in total 20 lifeboats, not much more than the number that was prescribed for a passenger and crew capacity of a 10,000 gross ton ship. Fourteen of those lifeboats had been constructed to carry 65 people each. The two emergency lifeboats could hold 40 people each and the four Engelhardt collapsibles, 47 people each. There were 2208 people on board, and room in the lifeboats for only 1178. Consequently, almost half of the passengers and crew were disadvantaged from the start.

Combine, then, this appalling lack of common sense with the fact that when *Titanic's* lifeboats left, they were filled to less than capacity. The average passenger load the boats were capable of carrying was 58.9; the average passenger load the boats actually carried was 32.6. Lifeboat number one, for example, could have held 40 people, but it left the *Titanic* with only 12. Similarly, while lifeboats numbered six and seven were capable of carrying 65 people each, they respectively left with 28 and 27 people. A total of only 652 people were loaded in the lifeboats.[1] Even though there were enough lifeboats to save over 50 percent of the people on the ship, less than one-third of the people left the *Titanic* that way.

During the investigations it was revealed that the ship's crew members had not received proper lifeboat drills. Why? Because there was no requirement by the Board of Trade that lifeboat drills be held.

It is easy, in hindsight, to highlight what at the beginning of the twenty-first century would be tantamount to criminal negligence. But was the Board of Trade criminally negligent? No. It was just complacent.

The British Board of Trade regulations had last been revised in 1894. At that time:

> The Merchant Shipping (Life Saving Appliances) Act, 1894, repealed the Act of 1888, and substituted therefore sections 427 to 431 and the seventeenth schedule of the new Act. Under this Act (1894), a table showing the minimum number of boats to be placed under davits, and their minimum cubic contents was issued by the Board. It was dated

---

1   *Report*, p. 39

the 9th of March, 1894, and came into operation on the 1st of June of that year. This table was based on the gross tonnage of the vessels to which it was to apply, and not upon the numbers carried, and it provided that the number of boats and their capacity should increase as the tonnage increased. The table, however, stopped short at the point where the gross tonnage of the vessels reached "10,000 and upwards." As to all such vessels, whatever their size might be, the minimum number of boats under davits was fixed by the table at 16, with a total minimum capacity of 5,500 cubic feet.[2]

Although the passenger-carrying capacity of ships built after 1894 greatly increased, the Board of Trade regulations, for a number of reasons, were not revisited. As Sir Alfred Chalmers, nautical advisor to the Board of Trade from 1896 to 1911, explained to the British enquiry, up until the time of the *Titanic*'s sinking, the record of transatlantic travel had been a clean one. Hundreds of ships carrying immigrants had travelled the routes without incident, and the routes themselves tended to be ones that both lessened the risk of collision and avoided ice and fog. Moreover, the ships being built around the turn of the century were stronger and better and therefore less likely to founder. Even if a ship were to encounter a disaster, Sir Alfred reasoned, it was believed that 16 lifeboats was the maximum number that could rapidly be dealt with at sea. As well, those experienced in the trade realized that in the event of an accident, particularly in inclement weather,

2   *Report*, p. 48

the ship that was sinking would have to rely on other ships in the vicinity for aid. Wireless telegraphy, introduced in 1901, provided the extra security that help could quickly be summoned if necessary.[3]

Then, as always, it took a tragedy to shake the world. Since that fateful night in 1912, and indeed as a result of it, much has changed with regard to safety at sea. Twenty-four recommendations ensued from the courts of inquiry; many were implemented. Without a doubt, many lives have been spared because of the increased safety standards that were a direct result of the *Titanic*'s sinking.

As the Board of Trade knew all along, however, a sufficient number of lifeboats and strictly enforced lifeboat drills will never guarantee safety of life on the sea. The *Titanic* was the exception, not the rule. Without the ideal weather conditions experienced the night it went down, many of those in the lifeboats would not have survived. In fact, it can be argued that so many did survive because the water was calm and the surface temperature did not seriously dip below freezing.

There have been numerous oceanic tragedies since the *Titanic*, and in none of these could the Board of Trade regulations be blamed. On May 28, 1914, the *Empress of Ireland*, after a collision with the Norwegian collier *Storstad*, sank in the St. Lawrence River, with a loss of over 1,000 lives. Almost one year later, on May 7, 1915, the world was shocked by the loss of the *Lusitania*, torpedoed off the coast of Ireland; 1,195 people died. On July 23, 1956, another 52 lives were lost, when the *Andrea Doria* collided with the Swedish ship *Stockholm* and sank off Nantucket. And the world reeled again, on February 15, 1982, long after we should have been safe on the sea,

---

3   *Report*, p. 49

when the oil rig *Ocean Ranger*, with a crew of 84, went down in the stormy waters of the Grand Banks of Newfoundland.

This is not to say that had the Board of Trade regulations in 1912 been stricter, the magnitude of the *Titanic*'s tragedy would not have been diminished. Undoubtedly it would have. With a sufficient number of lifeboats and proper lifeboat drills, and given the ideal weather conditions that prevailed, most, if not all, of *Titanic*'s passengers and crew would have stood an excellent chance of survival. It is simply to say that in hindsight many things become clear. The unsinkable ship was sinkable, other ships in the vicinity could not be counted upon to quickly come to its aid, and wireless telegraph was not the panacea it was believed to be. In other words, regulations that were perfectly acceptable up to April 14, 1912, were suddenly shown to be woefully inadequate.

GIVING
S.S. CALIFORNIAN'S
CAPTAIN LORD
HIS DUE

Was the *Titanic* beyond your range of vision? –
I should think so; 19½ or 20 miles away.

— *Captain Lord to the American Inquiry*

In the aftermath of the tragedy, the position of the freighter *Californian* and its proximity to the *Titanic* received considerable debate. So, too, did the role of Captain Stanley Lord, the *Californian*'s master.

S.S. *Californian*

The controversy began with statements made to the American press by Ernest Gill, second donkeyman on the *Californian*. For his efforts, Gill was paid $500 and received an invitation to the American inquiry.

Gill testified to the inquiry that on April 14 he was on duty in the engine room from 8 p.m. until midnight. The *Californian*'s engines had been stopped since 10:30 p.m. that evening, and she had been drifting amid floe ice. At five minutes to 12 he left the engine room and went on deck. It was "four minutes after 12, exactly," he stated, when he noticed from the deck on the starboard side "the lights of a very large steamer about 10 miles away." When he went below, he told his mate about the steamer, which he described as "going along full speed." About half an hour later, finding he could not sleep, Gill returned to the deck to smoke a cigarette. He told the inquiry it was then, at 12:30 a.m., that he saw "a white rocket about 10 miles away," followed seven or eight minutes later by another. Because he did not consider it his business to notify the bridge or the lookouts, he turned in, confident the ship would take any action that was necessary.

Gill continued his testimony by saying he was first aware of the sinking of the *Titanic* at 6:40 a.m. the next morning. From the conversations he had overheard and because of what he had witnessed himself, he was convinced that the ship he had seen in the early hour of the morning was the *Titanic*. Furthermore, he informed the inquiry, he believed others on the ship had seen the rockets and the captain had been made aware of them. Most damaging of all, he insinuated that Captain Lord had taken steps to cover up the *Californian*'s lack of action in the face of the tragedy.

Gill's story was the counterpart to the stories that had emerged from some of the *Titanic* survivors. Many of them, including the *Titanic's* Fourth Officer Boxhall, spoke of seeing the lights of an unidentified ship that was about five miles away. A number of survivors testified that they had been ordered by the officers of the *Titanic* to row towards the lights once they were safely aboard the lifeboats. Gill's story added an impetus to the emerging scandal that a ship had been in close range of the *Titanic* but had done nothing to help. That the ship they suspected was of the Leyland Line, controlled by the *Titanic's* parent company, seemed to make matters even worse.

To some extent Gill's testimony could be discounted. Whatever ship he had seen "going along full speed" at "four minutes after 12, exactly," it was certainly not the *Titanic*, since the *Titanic* had been stopped since 11:40 p.m. Nevertheless, as a result of Gill's allegations, Captain Lord and his crew were called to the inquiries to answer.

Their testimonies revealed that on the night of the disaster, the *Californian* stopped at the edge of an ice field at 10:21 p.m. Her position, as agreed to by all the officers, was then 42° 5′ N, 50° 7′ W. Ice stretched northward and southward, as far as the eye could see. While the *Californian* was stationary, at about 11 p.m., a vessel's lights could be seen in the distance, some seven to ten miles away. This vessel approached the *Californian*, her lights increasingly more visible, and stopped sometime around 11:30 p.m., approximately five miles off. Around 1 a.m. the first of a series of rockets was seen coming from the direction of the ship. Captain Lord, who had gone below to rest, was notified at quarter past one about the rockets. He instructed his second officer, Herbert Stone, to contact the mystery ship by Morse lamp. This was done repeatedly, with no reply, and then she disappeared bearing south west half west. Mr Stone described it as "a gradual disappearing of all her lights, which would be perfectly natural with a ship steaming away from us."[1] Throughout the night, Lord had remained in his cabin below and had not come on deck to personally investigate the matter.

The inquiries seized upon the evidence. Using what appeared to be reverse logic, they deduced that since the ship seen by the *Californian* appeared to have sent up rockets and the *Titanic* sent up rockets before she sank, the ship seen by the *Californian* had to be the *Titanic*. As Lord Mersey put it:

> ... the truth of the matter is plain. The *Titanic* collided with the berg at 11:40 p.m. The vessel seen by the *Californian* stopped at this time. The rockets sent up from the *Titanic* were distress signals. The *Californian* saw distress signals. The number sent up by the *Titanic* was about eight. The *Californian* saw eight. The time over which the rockets from the *Titanic* were sent up was from about 12:45 a.m. to 1:45 o'clock. It was about this time that the *Californian* saw the rockets. At 2:40 a.m. Mr Stone called to the Master that the ship from which he had seen the rockets had disappeared. At 2:20 a.m. the *Titanic* had foundered. It was suggested that the rockets seen by the *Californian* were from some other ship, not the *Titanic*. But no other ship to fit this theory has ever been heard of. These circumstances convince me that the ship seen by the *Californian* was the *Titanic* ...[2]

1   British enquiry, p. 45
2   British enquiry, pp. 45–46

It is quite possible there was a ship about five miles from the *Titanic* while the lifeboats were being lowered. There is no doubt there was a steamer within sight – some five to six miles distant according to the witnesses; eight to ten miles away in Lord Mersey's estimation – of the *Californian* the night the *Titanic* sank. It is known that the *Titanic* sent up rockets, and by all accounts rockets were seen coming from the direction of the ship being observed by the *Californian*. But to conclude from the testimonies of those before the inquiries that the *Titanic* and the *Californian* were in sight of each other is wrong. Quite simply, the stories that emerged at the inquiries differed to such an extent it should have been impossible to reach any conclusion about the proximity of the *Titanic* to the *Californian* on the night in question.

The *Californian's* third officer, Groves, was officer of the watch from 8 p.m. until midnight. Along with Captain Lord he navigated the freighter until she stopped at the ice edge at 10:21 p.m. At about 11:10 p.m., he observed a vessel, showing one masthead light, approaching from about 10 to 12 miles away, about three and a half points abaft the starboard beam, on a compass bearing of about south half west. Captain Lord, on the other hand, noticed a vessel at about 11 p.m., ten minutes earlier than Groves first noticed one, approaching from the eastward. Presumably it was the same vessel, although Groves's testimony had it coming from the south half west, whereas Lord's testimony had it coming from the east.

Groves further testified that at about 11:25 p.m., as the ship came nearer, he saw two masthead lights and her red (port) side light; he never saw her green (starboard) light. He noticed that she had changed her bearing more to the south and west and that she was approaching obliquely at about a 45-degree angle to the *Californian*, which, it must be noted, is a nautical impossibility. In contrast, Captain

Lord stated that when the ship was about five miles off, sometime between 11 and 11:30 p.m., he saw her green (starboard) side light and one masthead light. Again, both witnesses had the vessel heading opposite ways. Second Officer Stone and Apprentice Gibson, who viewed the ship at 12:20 a.m., also testified to seeing the vessel's red (port) side light and one masthead light, along with two or three indistinct lights, and gave the ship's direction as bearing about south south east by compass.[3]

The size of the steamer in the line of sight also received considerable debate. Groves told the British enquiry that the ship he was watching had a lot of deck lights and that there was no doubt in his mind that she was a passenger steamer. He testified that he had made a remark to this effect to the captain, who replied that she did not look like a passenger ship to him. At the hearings, Captain Lord emphatically denied the steamer was of a size to have been the *Titanic*; she was, he stated, a "medium size steamer." Stone and Gibson agreed with the captain. Stone testified that the vessel they were watching was "a smallish steamer" and followed up his statement by saying "Not the *Titanic*, by any means."[4] Gibson referred to her as a "tramp steamer."[5] Nevertheless, the inquiries,

---

3   Although there is a reasonable explanation for the differences in the testimony, to the best of my knowledge the courts of inquiry made no real attempt to find it. The most plausible reason that Captain Lord saw the starboard side light and the other officers saw the port side light is that they viewed the ship at different times and, in the case of Captain Lord and Third Officer Groves, perhaps only minutes apart. Furthermore, the scenario is quite consistent with a ship encountering the edge of pack ice, stopping, and turning her heading another way. It should be remembered that when the *Californian* encountered the pack ice, Captain Lord turned her heading to the east north east. This other ship, in all probability, also turned to an easterly heading after Captain Lord had seen her, thus then making her port side light visible to the other officers on the *Californian*. As for Stone and Gibson's testimony that at 12:20 a.m. the ship was bearing S S E by compass, this would indicate that the vessel was still stopped and heading eastward.

4   British enquiry, 8088, 8089

5   British enquiry, 7545

determined to reach the conclusion that it was the *Titanic*, dismissed the conflicting evidence, apparently using the logic that since the *Titanic* was a large passenger steamer, all the officers who did not see a large passenger steamer must have been mistaken.

The testimony from the *Titanic* survivors about the mystery ship they saw was even more inconsistent than that of the *Californian* crew. Hitchens, for example, related to the American inquiry that while he was in the lifeboat, he and his fellow passengers rowed towards a light, which, he said, "we expected to be a 'codbanker', a schooner that comes out on the Banks."[6] By the time of the British enquiry, he was referring to the lights as belonging to a steamboat, although under cross-examination he backtracked, saying "We expected it to be a steamer from the ship, but when I got into the boat and could not get near to it…then we expected it to be a fishing boat, a cod-banger (sic), as we call it."[7] Pitman told the British enquiry that he thought the white light was the stern light of a sailing vessel, while Lee said it could have been the light of one of their own boats. Lightoller was simply indecisive about what the light belonged to. He told the British enquiry:

> I knew there was…this light on the port bow about two points; I had already been calling many of the passengers' attention to it, pointing it out to them and saying there was a ship over there, that probably it was a sailing ship as she did not appear to come any closer…[8]

---

6   American inquiry, p.451
7   British enquiry, 1339
8   British enquiry, 13894

But when he was questioned again, he admitted he did not know the source of the light, or even how many lights there were:

> ...whether it was one or two lights I could not say. As to whether it was a mast-head light or a stern light, I could not say. I was perfectly sure it was a light attached to a vessel, whether a steamship or a sailing ship I could not say. I could not distinguish any other coloured lights, but merely it was a white light, distinct and plain.[9]

Boxhall, however, was more definite in his testimony.

He specified that on the night of the sinking, while lifeboats were being lowered, he and Captain Smith observed a vessel approaching almost end-on and first saw the navigating lights when the ship was about five miles off. At first, although he could see a light with the naked eye, he was unable to define it. Then, with the aid of binoculars, he discovered two masthead lights of a steamer, probably about half a point (5°) on the port bow; in this position the steamer under observation would have shown her red (port) side light if it had not been too far off to be visible. Boxhall recalled that he then paid particular attention to the vessel and that as she approached, he saw her side lights, her green light and red. At this point, he stated, the ship was end-on to the *Titanic*, steering straight towards them.

The fourth officer went on to say that as the ship came closer, he could see her red light and masthead lights with his naked eye. He judged her to be about five or six miles

---

9   British enquiry, 14138

away when he sent her a Morse signal, which went unanswered. The ship, he stated, then turned away – very, very slowly – until at last he saw only her stern light. She was headed, he said, in a "westerly direction" and confirmed for the inquiry that it was "almost in the direction from which she had come."[10]

Assuming for a moment that the light or lights those in the lifeboats were rowing towards and the lights Boxhall recounted seeing from the deck belonged to the same ship, it still remains to be explained how that ship could possibly have been the *Californian*. Boxhall's description of the ship's movements fits a description of a ship coming from the westward, proceeding slowly through pack ice, and then turning westward again. That ship could not possibly have been the *Californian*, because the *Californian* was stopped at the time to the northward and remained almost stationary until 5:15 in the morning.

Just as the inquiries failed to take proper note of the inconsistencies in the stories of the ships that were seen, they failed to take proper note of the ship that was not seen, or at least not seen until the *Titanic*'s lifeboats were being lowered and sent away. As Mr C. Roberston Dunlop, counsel for Leyland Line, attempted to point out at the British enquiry, neither Fleet nor Lee, the lookouts on the *Titanic*, reported the sighting of any ship on the horizon while they were in the crow's nest between the hours of 10 and 12 p.m. George Hogg, who relieved them

---

10 No one on either of the inquiries specifically questioned Fourth Officer Boxhall, whose expertise in celestial navigation enabled him to readily determine directions, about the direction the *Titanic* was heading in when he saw the lights of the mystery ship, five degrees on the port bow, coming directly towards them. Nevertheless, his testimony at the American inquiry (pages 909–11 and 914) and the British enquiry (page 336) clearly states that the ship observed was coming from the west, turned, and steamed away to the west again. Therefore, it is only logical that the *Titanic* was also heading in a westerly direction.

at midnight and stayed in the crow's nest until he was called to go away in the lifeboat, also did not see any lights of a steamer. In ordinary circumstances it is inconceivable, in the particular circumstances preposterous, that the bridge would not have been notified if a ship had been within sight between the time of the accident and the loading of the boats. Since the *Californian* had stopped in the ice at 10:21 p.m., it is also inconceivable that the lookouts would not have noticed her if, indeed, she was, as Lord Mersey asserted, only eight to 10 miles away.

As any solicitor will tell you, when establishing the facts of a case, one must look at what is logical and possible in order to get a clear picture of what actually transpired.

In this regard and with all due respect, the inquiries failed to properly consider in the first place whether the ship seen by the *Californian* could possibly have been the *Titanic*.

Granted, in buttressing his arguments that the ship in the *Californian*'s line of sight was the *Titanic*, Lord Mersey did refer to the ships' respective positions at the time of the sinking. He said in his report:

> The *Californian* proceeded on her course S 89° W true until 10:20 p.m., ships' time, when she was obliged to stop and reverse engines because she was running into field ice, which stretched as far as could then be seen to the northward and southward.
>
> The master told the Court that he made her position at that time to be 42° 5′ N, 57° 7′ W. This position is recorded in the log book, which was written up from the scrap log book by the chief officer. The scrap log is destroyed. It is a position about 19 miles N by E of the

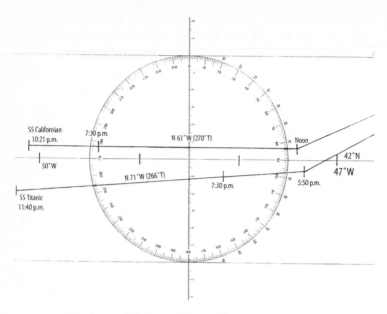

Tracks (path followed) by *Californian* and *Titanic*

position of the *Titanic* when she foundered, and is said to have been fixed by dead reckoning and verified by observations. I am satisfied that this position is not accurate.[11]

The report is obviously in error, and Lord Mersey's comment that he was satisfied the position was not accurate is rather ambiguous. Captain Lord did not tell the British enquiry that his ship's position at 10:20 p.m. was 42° 5′ N, 57° 7′ W. He told the enquiry it was 42° 5′ N, 50° 7′ W. The position of 57° 7′ W is not accurate, and it would have placed the *Californian* 309 miles west from where the *Titanic* foundered.

---

11 *Report*, p.43

Even if Lord Mersey meant to say "50° 7′ W′" or there was an error in transcription, his conclusion that the *Titanic* was only eight to 10 miles away from the *Californian* is not logical, as evidenced by the respective positions of the ships up to and including the night of the sinking.

The *Californian* was on a voyage from London to Boston. She was following the great circle track from Bishop's Rock to alter-course position 42° N, 47° W and then the rhumb line track to Boston. Her noon position on April 14 was 42° 05′ N, 47° 25′ W; her course was N 61° W by compass (west true) for Boston. The pole star sight at 7:30 p.m. revealed the latitude to be 42° 05′ N, which showed that she was making good her course of 270° true. The ship's speed was between 11 and 12 knots before she stopped at 10:21 p.m. There is no record in the *Californian's* log that she altered her course between 7:30 p.m. and 10:21 p.m., nor was any suggestion made afterwards that her course was in fact altered between these times.

The *Titanic* was on her maiden voyage from Queenstown to New York. She was following the great circle track from Fastnet Rock to alter-course position 42° N, 47° W and then the rhumb line track to New York. At about 5 p.m. on April 14 she was near 42° N, 47° W, on a course south 62° west true. She kept to this course until 5:50 p.m., when she altered her course to south 86° west true for New York.

That day, April 14, the weather conditions were ideal for fixing positions at noon and at 7:30 p.m. Officers of both ships, as did all ships' officers in the vicinity, fixed their positions at 7:30 p.m. by stellar observations. It is inconceivable that during the short steaming time, from 7:30 p.m. until 10:21 p.m. (two hours and 51 minutes), when the *Californian* stopped at the ice edge, and 11:46 p.m. (four hours and 16 minutes), when the *Titanic* stopped after impacting the ice, there would have been any significant errors in their respective DR positions. By this reasoning, then, the distance between the two vessels was about 19 to 20 miles, bearing south 15° west – north 15° east. This is approximately the distance of 15 miles you would expect to find at the 50th meridian of longitude between a vessel bound to New York, as the *Titanic* was, and a vessel bound to Boston, as the *Californian* was, if both were steering the course to the port to which each was respectively bound.

The *Californian's* Chief Officer Stewart said in evidence that the position of the *Californian* was fixed by stellar observation at 7:30 p.m. on Sunday evening, April 14. When the ship, surrounded by ice, stopped at 10:21 p.m., the captain calculated her position to be

Captain Lord and his officers

42° 05' N, 50° 07' W. This position, Stewart testified, he verified the next day. It was stated that all officers took sights, and Mr Stewart remarked during the hearings that all agreed with the positions that were entered into the ship's log.

The *Titanic*'s Fourth Officer Boxhall was confident at the hearings, and indeed until the end of his life, that his position, 41° 46' N, 50° 14' W, was correct.

Therefore, logical reasoning substantiates that at the time of the sinking, the *Titanic*'s position was 41° 46' N, 50° 14' W and that of the *Californian* was 42° 05' N, 50° 07' W – a distance of 19¹/₂ miles.

The technical experts at the hearings, who were presumably providing advice to the committees, also failed to appreciate the following:

1   The geographic range is the maximum distance at which the curvature of the earth and terrestrial refraction permit a light to be seen from a particular height of eye without regard to luminous intensity of the light.

2   The luminous range is the maximum distance at which a light can be seen under existing visibility conditions. This luminous range takes no account of the elevation of the light, the observer's height of eye, the curvature of the earth, or interference from background lighting. The luminous range is determined from the nominal range and the existing visibility conditions, using the Luminous Range Diagram.

3   The maximum range at which a light may be seen is the lesser of the luminous or geographic ranges.

4   The condition of the atmosphere has a considerable effect upon a light's range. Refraction may cause a light to be seen farther than under ordinary

circumstances. For a given candlepower, white is the most visible colour, green less so, and red the least of these.

5   Regardless of the height of eye, one cannot see a weak light beyond a certain luminous range.[12]

Given this, at 19½ miles apart, could the *Californian* and *Titanic* observers have seen each other's navigating lights, Morse lights, and deck lights? The answer is no.

As every competent deck officer knows, ships' Navigating lights cannot be seen beyond their luminous range.

Third Officer Groves's testimony held considerable sway over the British enquiry. It was he, of all the officers on the *Californian*, who emphatically stated that the ship whose navigating lights he saw was the *Titanic*. His assertion, however, simply does not stand up to scrutiny. He agreed with the captain and the other officers that when the *Californian* stopped, her position was 42° 05′ N, 50° 07′ W. He also knew by the time of the enquiry that the CQD position of the *Titanic* was 41° 46′ N, 50° 14′ W. He agreed that these positions made the distance between the *Titanic* and the *Californian* to be 19 to 20 miles. And he did not dispute that at a distance of 19 to 20 miles it would have been impossible to see the *Titanic*'s navigating and deck lights. He also acknowledged, under cross-examination by Mr Dunlop, that if the positions of the *Titanic* and the *Californian* as given were accurate, his opinion that the ship that was stopped some five miles away was the *Titanic* was wrong.

12 Bowditch, Nathaniel, LL.D., (1773-1838). *The American Practical Navigator.* Maryland: Defense Mapping Agency Hydrographic/Topographic Center, 1995, p. 54.

More damaging and erroneous evidence came from Captain John Knapp, a United States Navy hydrographer in charge of the Hydrographic Office of the Bureau of Navigation of the Navy Department. Testifying on the seventeenth day of the American hearings and armed with charts and hypotheses, he methodically argued, based on a hypothetical position of the *Californian*[13], that *Titanic* and the *Californian* were in sight of each other. He further suggested that the *Californian*, had she made the effort, could have reached the *Titanic* in sufficient time to save the lives of those on board.

In reference to a chart entitled "*Memorandum On Chart – Titanic –* Ice Barrier – Near-by Ships," he erroneously explained in much technical detail the theory of the visibility of lights. In particular, he noted that "16 miles represents the distance at which the side lights of the *Titanic* could be seen from one standing on the *Californian* at the height of the latter ship's side lights, or the reverse...."[14] Later, in reply to a question from Senator William Smith – "What do these arcs mean?" – Knapp stated:

> "The outer arc around each ship is drawn with a radius of 16 miles, which is approximately the farthest distance at which the curvature of the earth would have permitted the side lights of the *Titanic* to be seen by a person at the height of the side lights of the *Californian*, or at which the side lights of the *Californian* would have been seen by a person at the height of the side lights of the *Titanic*."[15]

---

13 Knapp's hypothetical position of the *Californian* was within a 16-mile radius of the *Titanic* at the time of the sinking. Not only was this misleading, but it suggests that evidence was being given to fit a predetermined conclusion.

14 American inquiry, p. 1118

15 American inquiry, p. 1119

What Knapp was detailing was the geographic range of the ship's side lights while ignoring the luminous intensity of these lights. *The maximum range at which lights may be seen is the lesser of the luminous or geographic ranges.* Therefore, if the geographic range, determined by height, is 16 miles and the luminous range is five miles, the lights are visible for five miles. At 19½ miles from the *Titanic*, those on board the *Californian* could not have seen her navigating lights.

Unfortunately for Captain Lord, the testimony of this expert witness, which was erroneous and misleading, damaged his reputation and ultimately helped to bring about his resignation from the *Californian*.

Although the courts of enquiry can be excused to some extent for relying on erroneous "expert" testimony, they cannot be excused for overlooking the obvious. In their rush to judgment against the *Californian*, they were no doubt aware that the 1912 Board of Trade regulations specified that the white masthead lights of vessels under way were to be of such a character as to be visible for at least five miles, the coloured side lights for at least two miles, and the stern light for at least one mile. They were also probably aware that in infinite visibility, the masthead lights could be seen for 10 miles and the side lights for three miles, but certainly no more than that. Working within this information, they apparently reasoned: "If the *Titanic* saw the lights of a ship and the *Californian* saw the lights of a ship, it was each other's lights they saw. If they saw each other's lights, they could have been no farther than 10 miles apart, because 10 miles would have been the maximum distance at which any of the lights could be seen."

What the inquiries did not take into account, however, is that since they supposedly saw each other's side lights, they could have been no further than three miles apart, which is preposterous given all the other evidence, and, more importantly, if they were close enough to have seen each other's navigating lights, they could not have failed to have seen each other's Morse signalling. Both ships were using powerful Morse lamps that were capable of being seen, given the infinite visibility that night, for a distance of at least 16 miles – farther than any of the navigating lights. Yet the evidence at the inquiries clearly established that the *Titanic* did not see the *Californian*'s Morse signals and the *Californian* did not see the *Titanic*'s. Why? Because they were not within viewing range of each other; they were more than 16 miles apart.

In spite of the inconsistencies and nonsensicalities, the inquiries pushed to their conclusions that the *Titanic* and the *Californian* were within sight of each other that night. For the most part the conclusions hinged on the testimony of the *Californian*'s crew about the rockets. Gill mentioned them to the American inquiry. Stone and Gibson, testifying at the British enquiry, stated that at about 12:55 a.m. they saw the first white flash in the sky immediately above the steamer they were observing. With the aid of binoculars, they saw four more white lights that had the appearance of white rockets bursting in the sky at intervals of about three or four minutes. Stone told the enquiry that at about 1:10 a.m. he notified the captain by voice tube that he had seen white lights in the sky. He said he took them to be white rockets and they were coming from the direction of the steamer. When the captain asked whether they were company signals, Stone replied that he did not know what they were. Although he held a First Mate Foreign-Going Certificate of Competency, for which, he testified, he had been examined "Last December twelve months," and had been to sea for eight years, he did not think the rockets were distress signals. [16]

The preponderance of evidence – the timing of the signals, the number of signals, the description of the signals, and the *Californian's* relative proximity to the *Titanic* – leads to the inevitable conclusion that the rockets were distress signals and that those signals were emanating from the White Star liner. This is not to say, however, that the *Titanic* and the *Californian* were within sight of each other. It is to say that at a distance of 19½ miles, the *Californian* would have had no difficulty seeing, and undoubtedly did see, the rockets sent up by the *Titanic*.

While the navigating lights, Morse, and deck lights of the *Titanic* and the *Californian* would have been out of the geographic and luminous ranges of each other, the distress signals sent up from the *Titanic's* bridge would have been within the geographic and luminous ranges because of their height above sea level and their high luminous intensity. At a height of 350 or more feet above sea level, or 290 feet above bridge level, and with a luminous intensity of 5000 candelas or more, the distress rockets would have been visible for a distance of at least 25 miles from the bridge of the *Titanic*, considering the infinite visibility that night.

---

16 Whether Second Officer Stone should have known they were distress signals is another matter. Article 31 of the 1912 Regulations for the Prevention of Collision at Sea states that "when a vessel is in distress and requires assistance from other vessels or from the shore, the following shall be the signals to be used or displayed by her either together or separately... At night, rockets or shells, throwing stars of any colour or description, fired one at a time, at short intervals." When Captain Lord asked Second Officer Stone whether they were coloured rockets, he replied that they were only "white" rockets. It seems Mr. Stone did not consider white rockets to be coloured distress rockets. The *Titanic's* Second Officer Lightoller, on the other hand, gave his description of an "actual distress signal" as "a shell [that] bursts at a great height in the air, throwing out a great number of stars... principally white, almost white."

The conclusion must be drawn that a ship some five miles distant from the *Californian* was in the line of sight of the *Titanic's* distress rockets. This hypothesis is given credence by Stone's testimony that he thought the rockets came from a greater distance past the ship because they did not seem to go very high and were only about half the height of the steamer's masthead lights. When later the ship was seen steaming towards the south west, she could very well have been steaming slowly through the ice towards the *Titanic's* position.

In all probability, the ship under observation by the *Californian* was not the ship whose lights were seen from the deck and lifeboats of the *Titanic*. If, as Boxhall said, that ship was close enough for her side lights to be seen, she was no more than three miles away. At three miles from the *Titanic's* port bow, her side lights would not have been visible to the *Californian*, which was more than 16 miles to the north. Even accepting the testimonies of those in the lifeboats that the ship's lights they were rowing towards were a good five miles off, that ship could not have been the one seen from the deck of the *Californian*. The concept of at least a second ship, also without Morse apparatus, between the *Titanic* and the *Californian* must therefore be entertained.

The courts of inquiry summarily dismissed the possibility of a third ship, and did not even consider the likelihood of a fourth, without Morse equipment, in the vicinity that night. The theory was not taken seriously simply because, as Lord Mersey noted, "no other ship to fit this theory has ever been heard of."[17]

It will probably never be known what ships lay between the *Titanic* and the *Californian* that night – the

---

17 Report of the British enquiry, p. 46

ship that was in the direct line of sight of the rockets, as well as the ship that offered false hope to the sinking liner. A few possibilities exist however.

The evidence shows there were three, possibly four, other steamers in the area. Their names are not known. At 5 a.m. the *Carpathia* saw two ships about five to six miles to the north of the *Titanic's* position; clearly, these two vessels were at this time in the neighbourhood where the *Titanic* went down. It may well have been that the steamer seen from the *Californian* was one of these two vessels, and it may well have been that the ship seen by the *Titanic's* Fourth Officer Boxhall was one of them. Shortly after 3 a.m., the *Mount Temple* also saw a sailing vessel coming from the direction in which the *Titanic* foundered; the *Mount Temple* was then some 15 to 16 miles from the *Titanic's* last position.

Lloyd's Weekly Shipping Index for the months of April and May, 1912, shows there were vessels at the time between the *Californian* and the *Titanic*.

One was the *Trautenfels*, belonging to the Hansa Line at Bremen. From the shipping index under the date May 2, 1912, it is noted that this ship, whose tonnage was 2,932, left Hamburg on March 31, bound for New York via Boston. On April 14 it is reported she was in latitude 42.1, longitude 49.53 when she encountered field-ice that extended for a distance of 30 miles and had to run the south west direction for 25 miles to clear it. Significantly, this ship was without Marconi apparatus and did what witnesses from the *Californian* described the ship they saw doing: she encountered ice and made a run to the south west. The *Trautenfels* arrived in Boston on April 18, en route to New York with residue cargo.

None of the ships sighted or listed by the index, including the *Trautenfels*, were investigated by either of the inquiries.

Yet another possibility exists for the mysterious fishing vessel whose lights were believed to have been seen by some of the *Titanic's* survivors. My personal research has revealed that on the morning of April 13, 1912, the 190-ton, three-masted tern schooner *Jean*, laden with 3694 quintals of salt fish, sailed with a fair wind from St. John's, Newfoundland, bound for Bahia, Brazil.[18] After rounding Cape Spear, her course to make good was 164 degrees true. This course coincided with the *Titanic's* CQD position, which also bore 164 degrees true, 360 miles from Cape Spear. At a speed of eight knots, the *Jean* would have been in the latitude of the *Titanic* early Monday morning, April 15, 1912. Significantly, she sailed without Marconi apparatus.

Critics of the mystery ships theory argue that if there had been one or more ships between the *Titanic* and the *Californian*, surely in the wake of the tragedy their officers would have come forward. Unfortunately, while common decency might demand it, reality would dictate otherwise. Those on a ship travelling without Marconi apparatus, as the ships sighted by the *Californian* and the *Titanic* evidently were, would not have been aware of the sinking until the ship put into port. It is unlikely that officers and crew of a foreign ship especially would believe themselves to be under any obligation to answer to a British or American inquiry, particularly if waiting around for an investigation meant lost wages and a delay in departure. And sadly enough, their testimony would do nothing to change the appalling fact that the *Titanic* had sunk with an incredible loss of life.

Thus Captain Lord alone was held accountable for the extent of the tragedy. Unfairly perhaps he was roundly

---

18   *The Evening Telegram*, St. John's, Newfoundland, April 13, 1912

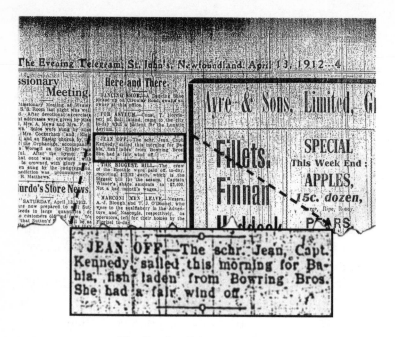

The Evening Telegram re Jean

condemned for going back to sleep after he had been notified of the rockets. Yet Lord did have reason to believe that the rockets were company signals. Quite often, ships of the same line communicated to each other by sending up rockets when they were within a certain distance at sea. The steamer the *Californian* had under surveillance was showing no signs of distress. That she was not answering the Morse lamp was no call for concern, because often ships called up by Morse lamp did not answer. Then, too, was Second Officer Stone's advice to him, relayed by Gibson at 1:15 a.m., that the vessel they had had in sight had "steamed away."[19]

19 British enquiry, 6895

A ship steaming away is a different sight from one that is sinking.

Nevertheless, Lord Mersey, in his summation of the *Californian's* role in the affair, bluntly said that if the *Californian* had pushed through the ice when she first saw the rockets, "she might have saved many if not all of the lives that were lost."[20] Shortly after the inquiries ended, Captain Lord was asked to resign as the master of the *Californian*.

His letter of August 10, 1912, to the Assistant Secretary of the Marine Department, was but the first of his many, unsuccessful, lifelong attempts to explain his actions on the night the *Titanic* foundered. His words are not without human logic:

> With regard to my own conduct on the night in question. I should like to add a little more. I had taken every precaution for the safety of my own ship and left her in charge of a responsible officer at 0:40 a.m., with instructions to call me if he wanted anything, and I lay down fully dressed. At 1:15 a.m. (25 minutes after he had seen the first signal) the officer on watch reported the steamer we had in sight was altering her bearing, in other words was steaming away, and had fired a rocket. I did not anticipate any disaster to a vessel that had been stopped nearby for an hour, and had ignored my Morse signals, and was then steaming away. I asked him was it a Co. [company] signal, and to signal her and let me know the result. It is a matter of great regret to

me that I did not go on deck myself at this time, but I didn't think it possible for any seaman to mistake a Co. signal for a distress signal, as I relied on the officer on watch.

Although further signals were seen between 1:15 a.m. and 2 a.m. I was not notified until 2 a.m., and then I had fallen into a sound sleep, and whatever message was sent to me then, I was not sufficiently awake to understand, and it was sufficient indication to anyone that I had not realized the message by the fact that I still remained below, curiosity to see a vessel pushing through the ice would have taken me on deck. The message sent to me at 2 a.m. was I heard later, to the effect that the steamer we had in sight at 11:30 p.m., had altered her bearing from S S E to S W ½ W[21] and had fired eight rockets, and was then out of sight...

Further signals were seen after 2 a.m. but the officer was so little concerned about them, that he did not think it necessary to notify me. I was called by the chief officer at 4:30 a.m., and in conversation he referred to the rockets seen by the second officer, I immediately had the wireless operator called, heard of the disaster, and proceeded at once, picking through field ice to the scene, and I would have done the same earlier had I understood, as I had everything to gain and nothing to lose.

---

21 To do this, she must have steamed eight miles. The *Titanic* did not move after midnight.

The facts remain that Captain Lord and the *Californian* did not respond to the *Titanic's* distress signals that night and, for this, he was vilified. His sin, however, was not indifference or complete disregard for human life. It was the transgression of the cardinal rule for the practice of good seamanship: when in doubt, never assume, always confirm. When Second Officer Stone reported seeing white rockets, Lord's duty as master of his ship was to immediately go to the bridge, investigate, and confirm. There was no justification for his having delegated this responsibility to a subordinate. Similarly, when the Morse signalling did not achieve the desired results, it was his responsibility to have the wireless operator called.

If these steps had been taken, Lord would not have been faulted, even though in the final analysis they would not have made a difference. His ship, which was stopped because of ice and darkness, was 19½ miles from the *Titanic*. Regardless of whether he had gotten under way at the first sighting of the rockets at 12:45 a.m. and proceeded at the fastest, safest speed, he could never have reached the *Titanic* before she sank.

TESTIMONY OF SHIPS SIGHTED
British Enquiry

Wreck Commissioners' Court
Wreck Commissioner of the United Kingdom &
Subcommittee of the Committee on Commerce
United States Senate

Mr Charles Victor Groves, *Sworn.*
Examined by Mr S.A.T. Rowlatt.

8112 Were you second officer of the *Californian*? –
Yes, I was on the ship's articles as second officer,
but took the duties of third.

8134 Did you see any ships approaching? – Yes.

8135 Now, what did you see, and when? – As I said
before, the stars were showing right down to the
horizon. It was very difficult at first to
distinguish between the stars and a light, they
were so low down. About 11:10, ship's time, I
made out a steamer coming up a little bit abaft
our starboard beam.

8143   What lights did you see? – At first I just saw
        what I took to be one light, but, of course, when
        I saw her first I did not pay particular attention
        to her, because I thought it might have been a
        star rising.

8146   Did you then see more lights than one? – About
        11:25. I made out two lights – two white lights.

8147   Two masthead lights? – Two white masthead
        lights.

8149   You said that she was a little abaft your
        starboard beam? – Yes.

8150   How were you heading? – At that time we
        would be heading NE when I saw that steamer
        first, but we were swinging all the time because
        when we stopped the order was given for the
        helm to be put hard-a-port, and we were
        swinging, but very, very slowly.

8151   You say you were heading about NE? – We were
        heading NE.

8152   Did you notice that at the time? – Yes.

8153   Was that with a view to see in what direction
        the steamer was bearing? – No, for my own
        information.

8154   But it was at that time? – At that time, yes.

8155   Now, how did she bear, how many points abaft
        the beam did she bear? – Do you mean when I
        first noticed her?

8156   Yes? – I should think about 3½ points, but I
        took no actual bearing of her.

8157   That would leave her S by W? – We were heading
         NE and she was three points abaft the beam.

8158   Your beam would be? – SE.

8159   That would bring her about 7? – S or S by W. –
         S ½ W.

It should be noted that Groves was unable to readily
determine the correct bearing. On a NE heading, three
and a half points abaft the starboard beam would
actually be S ½ E.

8160   Could you form any judgment how far off she
         was? – When I saw her first light I should think
         she would be about 10 or 12 miles.

8161   Judging by the look of the light? – By the look
         of the light and the clearness of the night.

8162   (*The Commissioner*) That was when you saw the
         one light? – Yes, when I say she was 10 to
         12 miles away.

8163   (*Mr Rowlatt*) Did she appear to get nearer? –
         Yes.

8164   The lights clearer? – Yes, all the time.

8165   Was she changing her bearing? – Slowly.

8166   Coming round more to the south and west? –
         More on our beam, yes, more to the south and
         west, but very little.

Groves's comment that the ship under observation was
coming "more on our beam" indicates that she was
steering east of north with her port side open, whereas
his comment "more to the south and west" indicates

she was steering west of north with her starboard side open. His testimony here is contradictory and nautically illogical.

8167   Did you report that to the captain? – Yes, because, as I said before, he left orders to let him know if I saw any steamers approaching.

8169   (*The Commissioner*) Would this be something after 11 o'clock? – Yes, My Lord, when I went down to him it would be as near as I could judge about 11.30.

8170   (*Mr Rowlatt*) What did you say to him? – I knocked at his door and told him there was a steamer approaching us coming up on the starboard quarter.

8172   (*Mr Rowlatt*) Did you say what sort of a steamer you thought she was? – Captain Lord said to me, "Can you make anything out of her lights?" I said, "Yes, she is evidently a passenger steamer coming up on us."

8176   (*Mr Rowlatt*) Did you say why you thought she was a passenger steamer? – Yes. I told him I could see her deck lights and that made me pass the remark that she was evidently a passenger steamer.

8178   (*Mr Rowlatt*) How many deck lights had she? Had she much light? – Yes, a lot of light. There was absolutely no doubt her being a passenger steamer, at least in my mind.

8179   Could you see much of her length? – No, not a great deal; because as I could judge she was coming up obliquely to us.

8180   She was foreshortened? – Supposing we were
        heading this way she would be coming up in this
        way perhaps an angle of 45 degrees to us
        (*demonstrating*).

8182   Now is that all you said to the captain before he
        said something to you? – Yes. He said, "Call her
        up on the Morse lamp, and see if you can get
        any reply."

8185   What did you say to that? – I went up on the
        bridge; I went away and went up on the bridge
        and I rigged the Morse lamp.

8188   (*Mr Rowlatt*) Did you get any reply? – Not at
        first, no reply whatsoever.

8189   Did you afterwards? – Well, what I took to be a
        reply. I saw what I took to be a light answering,
        and then I sent the word "What?" meaning to
        ask what ship she was. When I sent "What?" his
        light was flickering. I took up the glasses again
        and I came to the conclusion it could not have
        been a Morse lamp.

8190   (*The Commissioner*) Is the long and short of it
        this, that you did not get a reply, in your
        opinion? – In my opinion, no.

The *Californian*'s Morse lamp was capable of being
seen 10 miles away in normal visibility, and possibly up
to 16 miles away given the infinite visibility of that
night. Those on the *Titanic* did not see the Morse light
from the *Californian*, or indeed from any ship. The
Titanic was also sending her Morse light, which was
capable of being seen at a distance of 16 miles, but it
was not observed from the *Californian*. Therefore, the

ship being watched by Groves could not possibly have been the *Titanic*.

8197   After that was done, did you have any more conversation with the captain about the steamer? – When he came up on the bridge he said to me, "That does not look like a passenger steamer." I said, "It is, Sir. When she stopped her lights seemed to go out, and I suppose they have been put out for the night."

8203   (*The Comissioner*) You said something about the lights of the ship going out. When did they go out? – At 11:40.

8217   (*Mr Rowlatt*) What makes you fix the time 11:40 for her lights going out? – Because that is the time we struck one bell to call the middle watch.

8218   Do you remember that bell was struck at that time? – Most certainly.

8219   Did the steamer continue on her course after that? – No, not so far as I could see.

8220   She stopped? – She stopped.

8221   Was that at the time when her lights appeared to go out? – That was at the time when her lights appeared to go out.

Were the lights you saw on her port side or on her starboard side? – Port side.

Since the vessel under observation had her port side deck light open, her heading must have been east of north, approximately NE.

8223   I want to ask you a question. Supposing the
        steamer whose lights you saw turned two points
        to port at 11:40, would that account to you for
        her lights ceasing to be visible to you? – I quite
        think it would.

        (*The Commissioner*) Mr Rowlatt, at 11:40 the
        engines were stopped on the *Titanic*.

        (*Mr Rowlatt*) Yes, my Lord.

**The *Titanic* was heading N 71° W compass at
11:40 p.m. when she turned two points to port for a
heading of S 86° W compass. The vessel Groves was
observing was heading, according to his testimony,
approximately NE compass.**

8227   Did you continue to see the masthead lights?
        – Yes.

8228   Did you see any navigation lights – side lights? –
        I saw the red port light.

8229   (*The Commissioner*) When did you see that? –
        As soon as her deck lights disappeared from
        my view.

8230   (*Mr Rowlatt*) Did it strike you that going out of
        the glare of the other lights could show up the
        port light? Is that what you mean? – Yes, it
        would do.

8232   I only want to understand. You cannot see a red
        light in the midst of the glare of the deck lights.
        That is what you mean? – Yes, because of the
        blaze of the white lights.

For the navigation lights to be obscured by a glare from the deck lights would be contrary to, and in violation of, the 1912 Board of Trade Regulations regarding navigation lights. Groves's answer demonstrated his lack of professional seamanship and knowledge.

8246   Was she keeping her same position? – The same position, yes. We were swinging slowly to port, very slowly.

8248   She would appear to be coming round more towards your stern? – No, she would appear, as we were swinging, to be working towards our head.

8249   I thought you were swinging to port? – No, we were swinging to starboard – that is to the right hand.

8250   How long did you stay on the bridge? – I stayed on the bridge till something between 12:10 and 12:15.

        (*Mr Rowlatt*) I was asking for information, my Lord, because I thought he had said before that he thought she had put her lights out because of the time of night.

8264   (*The Commissioner – To the Witness*) Did you say that you thought she had put her lights out because of the time of night? – I did say that, I think, my Lord.

8265   Then which is it to be, that she shut them out because she was changing her position, or that she had put them out because, in your opinion it was bed-time on board the ship? – Well, at the time the lights disappeared I thought in my own mind she had put them out because in the ships I was accustomed to before I joined this company it was the custom to put all the deck lights out, some at 11 p.m., some at 11:30, and some at midnight – all the deck lights except those absolutely necessary to show the way along the different decks. But when I saw the ice I came to the conclusion that she had starboarded to escape some ice.

8266   You came to the conclusion then, did you, while you were on the bridge? – Yes, my Lord.

Examined by Mr Scanlan.

8384   You said when you first saw the ship she appeared to be about 10 miles from you? – Ten to twelve, I said.

8385   When she came to a stop what was the distance? – Well, I should think about five to seven miles.

Examined by Mr Holmes.

8419   What is the average range of an ordinary ship's side light? – Two miles.

8420   And the mast head light? – Five miles; that is the distance they are supposed to show.

8421   They do show a little further on a clear night? – Yes.

Examined by Mr Robertson Dunlop.

8425   In the log book it is stated that when you stopped your ship in the ice the position of the ship was 42° 5′ N and longitude 50° 7′ W. Is that accurate? – Well, it is bound to be accurate if the captain put it in.

8440   If this vessel which you did see was only some four or five miles to the southward of you, do you think she could have been the *Titanic*?

8441   (*The Commissioner*) That is a question I want this witness to answer. (*To the Witness*) Speaking as an experienced seaman and knowing what you do know now, do you think that steamer that you know was throwing up rockets, and that you say was a passenger steamer, was the *Titanic*? – Do I think it?

8442   Yes? – From what I have heard subsequently?

8443   Yes? – Most decidedly I do, but I do not put myself as being an experienced man.

8444   But that is your opinion as far as your experience goes? – Yes, it is, my Lord.

(*Mr Robinson Dunlop*) That would indicate that the *Titanic* was only four or five miles to the southward of the position in which you were when you stopped.

If Groves saw the red port side light of the ship under observation, she must have been no further away than three miles, since the maximum range of visibility for a side light is three miles.

8445   (*Mr Robinson Dunlop*) You will appreciate, Mr
         Groves, that if the latitudes are right it follows
         that your opinion must be wrong? – If the
         latitudes are right, then of course I am wrong.

8446   If the latitude of your ship and that of the
         Titanic are anything approximately right, it
         follows that the vessel which you saw could not
         have been the *Titanic*? – Certainly not.

8451   What, apart from the masthead lights, was there
         to indicate to you that this was a large passenger
         steamer? – The number of deck lights she was
         showing.

8455   That being so, how did those deck lights
         communicate to you that this was a large
         passenger steamer? – Well, as I said before, by
         the number of her lights; there was such a glare
         from them.

**The glare from the lights that Groves referred to was a
result of abnormal refraction.**

8465   Before the vessel which you saw stopped, on
         what course did she seem to you to be steering?
         – Do you mean the steamer I had seen at 11:40?

8466   Yes, before she stopped at 11:40 you had had her
         under observation for some time, noticing her
         movements? – Yes, but I took no notice of the
         course she was making except that she was
         coming up obliquely to us.

**Here Groves contradicted the answer he gave in
Question 8180.**

8467   Was she making to the westward or to the
        eastward? – She would be bound to be going
        westward.

8468   Was she? – She was bound to.

8469   Did you see her going westward? – Well, I saw
        her red light.

8470   If she was going to the westward and was to the
        southward of you, you ought to have seen her
        green light? – Not necessarily.

8471   Just follow me for a moment. She is coming up
        on your starboard quarter, you told us? – On our
        starboard quarter.

8472   Heading to the westward? – I did not say she
        was heading to the westward.

8473   Proceeding to the westward? – Yes.

8474   And she is to the southward of you? – She is to
        the southward of us.

8475   Then the side nearest to you must have been
        her starboard side, must it not? – Not
        necessarily. If she is going anything from N to
        W you would see her port light. At the time I
        left the bridge we were heading E N E by
        compass.

8476   Never mind about your heading. I am only
        dealing with her bearings. She is bearing S S E
        of you – south easterly? – About south.

8477   She is south of you and apparently proceeding
        to the westward? – Yes, some course to the
        westward.

8478   Does it follow from that that the side that she
        was showing to you at that time must have been
        her starboard side? – No, it does not follow at
        all. If she is steering a direct west course, yes.

8479   Did you see her green light at all? – Never.

Groves's evaluation of the ship's direction is nautically
illogical.

Frederick Fleet, *Sworn.*
Examined by Mr Scanlan.

17428   (*Mr Scanlan – To the Witness*) Now I want to ask
        you this question. Before you left the *Titanic* did
        you observe the lights of any ship in your
        neighbourhood? – Well, there was a light on the
        port bow.

17429   Did you see this light on the port bow before
        you left the crow's nest? – No, it must have been
        about 1 o'clock.

Reginald Robinson Lee, *Sworn.*
Examined by the Attorney-General.

2364   You were the lookout man? – Yes.

2419   Before half-past eleven on that watch – that is,
        seven bells – had you reported anything at all,
        do you remember? – There was nothing to be
        reported.

2420   Then what was the first thing you did report? – The first thing that was reported was after seven bells struck; it was some minutes, it might have been nine or 10 minutes afterwards. Three bells were struck by Fleet, warning, "Right ahead," and immediately he rung the telephone up to the bridge, "Iceberg right ahead." The reply came back from the bridge, "Thank You."

(*The Commissioner*) This would be about 11:40.

2564   When the steamer struck, was there any light of any other vessel to be seen? – No.

George Alfred Hogg, *Sworn.*
Examined by the Attorney-General.

17525   On this particular night, Sunday the 14th, when the collision happened, your mate was Evans, was he not? – Yes.

17526   You were not on duty – you did not go on duty till 12 o'clock? – Twelve.

17527   That is right? – That is right.

17528   You relieved Fleet and Lee? – Yes.

17559   When you went to relieve them at 12 o'clock, was anything said to you then? – Nothing was passed on to us at all then.

If the *Californian* had been stopped three miles to the north of the *Titanic*, surely she and her Morse signalling would have been seen by the lookouts and reported.

TESTIMONY OF SHIPS SIGHTED

American Inquiry

Testimony of Joseph Groves Boxhall (Recalled)

Senator Smith: You were the fourth officer on the *Titanic*?

Mr Boxhall: Yes, sir.

Senator Smith: I understood you to say that you saw a steamer almost ahead of you, or saw a light that night, about the time of the collision?

Mr Boxhall: Shortly afterwards; yes, sir.

Senator Smith: Did you describe that light? What was the character of the light you saw; and did you see more than one?

Mr Boxhall: At first I saw two masthead lights of a steamer, just slightly opened, and later she got closer to us, until, eventually, I could see her side lights with my naked eye.

Senator Smith: Was she approaching you?

Mr Boxhall: Evidently she was, because I was stopped.

Senator Smith: And how far away was she?

Mr Boxhall: I considered she was about five miles away.

Senator Smith: In which direction?

Mr Boxhall: She was headed toward us, meeting us.

Senator Smith: Was she a little toward your port bow?

Mr Boxhall: Just about half a point off our port bow.

Senator Smith: And apparently coming toward you?

Mr Boxhall: Yes.

Senator Smith: And how soon after the collision?

Mr Boxhall: I can not say about that. It was shortly after the order was given to clear the boats.

Senator Smith: Did you continue to see that steamer?

Mr Boxhall: I saw that light, saw all the lights of course, before I got into my boat, and just before I got into the boat she seemed as if she had turned around. I saw just one single bright light then, which I took to be her stern light.

Senator Smith: She apparently turned around within five miles of you?

Mr Boxhall: Yes, sir.

Senator Smith: Had the rockets then gone off on the *Titanic?*

Mr Boxhall: Yes, sir. I had been firing off rockets before I saw her side lights. I fired off the rockets and then she got so close I could see her side lights and starboard light.

Senator Smith: What kind of steamer was that which you saw, that apparently turned around, as to size and character?

Mr Boxhall: That is hard to state, but the lights were on masts which were fairly close together – the masthead lights.

Senator Smith: What would that indicate?

Mr Boxhall: That the masts were pretty close together. She might have been a four-mast ship or might have been a three-mast ship, but she certainly was not a two-mast ship.

Senator Smith: Could you form any idea as to her size?

Mr Boxhall: No, I could not.

Senator Smith: You know it was a steamer and not a sailing vessel?

Mr Boxhall: Oh, yes; she was a steamer, carrying steaming lights – white lights.

Senator Smith: She could not have been a fishing vessel?

Mr Boxhall: No, sir.

Senator Smith: Was she a sailing vessel?

Mr Boxhall: No, sir; a sailing vessel does not show steaming lights, or white lights.

Senator Smith: After you got in the water did you see the light from this steamer that you had seen previously?

Mr Boxhall: Yes; I saw it for a little while and then lost it. When I pulled around the ship I could not see it any more, and did not see it any more.

Senator Smith: Apparently that ship came within four or five miles of the *Titanic*, and then turned and went away in what direction, westward or southward?

Mr Boxhall: I do not know whether it was southwestward. I should say it was westerly.

Senator Smith: In a westerly direction; almost in the direction from which she had come?

Mr Boxhall: Yes, sir.

Fourth Officer Boxhall held an extra master's certificate of competency. His expertise in celestial navigation enabled him to readily determine the direction in which the *Titanic* was heading when the lights of the ship under observation were five degrees on the port bow, pointing directly at the *Titanic*. His evidence was that this ship was coming from the west, turned, and steamed away to the west again. Therefore, it is only logical that the *Titanic* was heading in a westerly direction. The *Californian* was to the northward, and therefore could not possibly have been the ship seen from the deck of the *Titanic*.

Senator Smith: You have had 13 years experience?

Mr Boxhall: Yes, sir.

Senator Smith: In navigation?

Mr Boxhall: Yes, sir.

Testimony of Mr Frederick Fleet

Senator Smith: Were there lights of any other vessels
                     in sight when you came down from the
                     crow's nest?

Mr Fleet: There was no lights at all when we was
                     up in the crow's nest. This is after we
                     was down and on the boats; then I seen
                     the light.

Senator Smith: I am not speaking of that. I wanted to
                     know whether you saw ahead, while
                     you were on the watch, on the lookout,
                     Sunday night, after the collision
                     occurred or before, any lights of any
                     other ship.

Mr Fleet: No, sir.

Senator Smith: You saw no lights at all?

Mr Fleet: No, sir.

Senator Smith: But you saw no lights ahead that
                     indicated the presence of another
                     vessel?

Mr Fleet: No, sir.

Senator Smith: Or while you were in the crow's nest?

Mr Fleet: No, sir.

Senator Smith: Nor any other object except the one
                    you have described?

Mr Fleet: No, sir.

TITANIC: LOST AND FOUND

Supporting Boxhall's CQD Position

One of the first things that Capt. Rostron said after I met him was, "What a splendid position that was you gave us."

— *Titanic's Fourth Officer Boxhall to the American Inquiry*

On September 1, 1985, an expedition led by Dr Robert Ballard located the wreckage of the *Titanic* on the ocean floor. Her position at the time of the discovery was 41° 43.9′ N, 49° 56.8′ W, some 13 miles east of where she had reportedly foundered.

The discovery opened the floodgates of controversy once again. Armchair navigators scrambled to explain the discrepancy and, in doing so, held the *Titanic's* distress position up to scrutiny.

Shortly after the impact with the ice, on April 14, 1912, it was the *Titanic's* Fourth Officer Boxhall who had calculated her CQD position. He had based his calculations on Second Officer Lightoller's six-star observation (three stars for latitude, three stars for longitude), taken at 7:30 that evening, and determined it to be 41° 46′ N, 50° 14′ W. Considering that the wreck was not found at this location, the obvious, and easy, conclusion is that Boxhall's position was wrong.

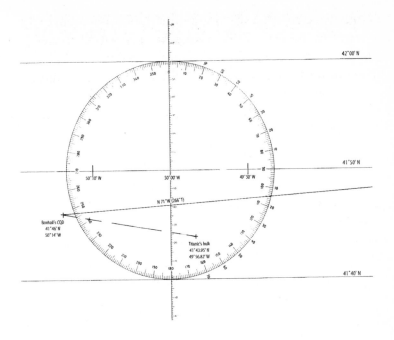

Titanic's hulk position relative to Boxhall's CQD position

Such a hasty conclusion, however, does disservice to Fourth Officer Boxhall. By all accounts, he was a competent officer. He was a professional mariner who had been at sea for 13 of his 28 years, five of which had been with the White Star Line, and he held an extra master certificate of competency. Moreover, as a competent officer, he would have had no difficulty in calculating his distress position based on the star sights Second Officer Lightoller had taken earlier that evening.

It is also highly unlikely that the 7:30 p.m. position derived from Lightoller's star observations was in error. The taking of sights on six different stars, to all intents and purposes, eliminates the possibility of error. There is also the fact that the weather conditions were ideal for fixing positions that day. Lightoller, too, was a competent navigating officer and held an extra master certificate of competency. There was no reason to doubt his star observations; they were, in Boxhall's estimation, beautiful sights – sharp and accurate.

It has been suggested that the *Titanic's* navigators overestimated her speed by roughly two knots and this in turn caused Boxhall to miscalculate his dead reckoning position at the time of the impact. This theory, as well, does not withstand closer examination.

The *Titanic's* position, like that of other ships in the vicinity, had been fixed at noon and 7:30 p.m. on April 14. Again, given the fine weather, it can be safely assumed that these positions were accurate. From noon until 7:30 p.m., when Second Officer Lightoller made his six-star observation, the *Titanic's* speed over ground[1] would have been established, irrespective of the log reading,[2] and any discrepancy between the actual distance travelled and the log reading would have been noted.

When the *Titanic* impacted the ice at 11:40 p.m., the log reading showed she had travelled 260 miles from the time of the noon log reset at an average speed through the water of 22¼ knots. Taking into account the effect of the Gulf Stream current, this would have made her speed over ground approximately 22 knots. For the last four hours and 10 minutes of that time (from 7:30 p.m. to 11:40 p.m.), she had been running on compass course north 71° west (south 86° west true). Navigational checks for any compass deviation would have been made routinely and the courses steered would have been monitored. There

---

1 "Speed over ground" is the vessel's actual speed, which is determined by dividing the distance between successive fixes by the time between the fixes.

2 The log is an instrument for measuring the speed and distance, or both, travelled by a vessel through the water and is usually reset to zero every noon.

were also no inclement weather conditions that would have affected her course. It is therefore inconceivable that on a run of four hours and 10 minutes, there would have been any significant error in the CQD position.

Significantly, the rescue by the *Carpathia* confirmed the accuracy of Fourth Officer Boxhall's position. Testifying at both the American and the British enquiries, Captain Rostron of the *Carpathia* affirmed that at about 12:25 a.m. his wireless operator had received a distress call from the *Titanic*, whose position was cited as 41° 46′ N, 50° 14′ W. Immediately upon hearing about the call, at 12:35 a.m., he picked up the *Carpathia's* position on the chart and set a course to pick up the *Titanic*. That course was, he stated, north 52 degrees west true, about 58 miles from the *Carpathia*. Proceeding on this course and after running his distance, he arrived at the *Titanic's* stated position shortly after 4 a.m. There he found the survivors, drifting in their lifeboats. Boxhall's lifeboat, number two, was the first to pull alongside the *Carpathia* and transfer the survivors. Captain Rostron was apparently direct in his praise. According to Fourth Officer Boxhall's testimony at the American inquiry, one of the first things the captain said upon greeting him was "What a splendid position that was you gave us."[3] Captain Rostron, as well, confirmed at the British enquiry that the position calculated by the fourth officer was correct.[4]

It is true that counter-evidence to the accuracy of Boxhall's position was provided by Captain James Moore of the Canadian Pacific Railway's *Mount Temple*. Moore, who had proceeded to the scene upon hearing of the disaster, testified at the American inquiry that the *Titanic's*

---

3   American inquiry, p. 931
4   British enquiry, 25551

CQD position was wrong. Her correct position, he maintained, was actually eight miles farther to the east. Moore's testimony, however, is too full of inconsistencies and contradictions to be supportable.

According to the evidence, on April 15, at 12:30 a.m., the *Mount Temple* received a general message saying: "*Titanic* sends C.Q.D. Requires assistance. Position 41° 44' North, longitude 50° 24' west. Come at once. Iceberg." Moore immediately ordered his ship to the rescue. Shortly after "turning around," though, the *Mount Temple* received a second set of co-ordinates, which this time gave the *Titanic*'s position as 41° 46' N, 50° 14' W. The latter position was the correct one.[5]

Moore at first testified that when the *Titanic*'s CQD was received, the *Mount Temple*'s position was 41° 25' N, 51° 15' W. After consulting a memorandum, however, he corrected himself, saying it was 41° 25' N, 51° 41' W – a difference of 19½ miles west of the previously stated position. He calculated that the *Titanic* was 49 miles from the *Mount Temple* and set his course at N 65° E true. Yet if the *Mount Temple* was 49 miles from the *Titanic*, then the first position Moore gave, from memory, was the correct one. A position of 41° 25' N, 51° 41' W would actually bring her 69 miles from the site of the sinking.

Moore also claimed to have arrived at the *Titanic*'s CQD position at 4:30 a.m. He stated in evidence that after receiving the distress call and verifying the positions, the *Mount Temple* set out, going at full speed of 11½ knots, although "perhaps a little bit of the Gulf Stream was with her too."[6] At 3 a.m., he said, they began to meet the ice, and at 3:25 a.m. they stopped. According to his

5   American inquiry, p. 760
6   American inquiry, p. 760

calculations, at that point he was about 14 miles off the *Titanic*'s position. He said: "I did not stop her altogether; I simply stopped the engines and let the way run off the ship and proceed slowly... I reached the *Titanic*'s position... at 4:30 a.m. in the morning."[7] The *Mount Temple*, however, could not have reached the site of the disaster by 4:30 a.m. At full speed she could run only 11½ knots – 12 knots with the current running with her – and in one hour and five minutes (from 3:25 a.m. to 4:30 a.m.), after stopping and proceeding slowly, she could not have travelled 14 nautical miles. In all likelihood, she travelled at most three to four miles.

Further inconsistent evidence comes from Moore's reported sightings of the *Carpathia* and the *Californian* that Monday morning and his position relative to them. To the American inquiry he stated:

> I suppose about 6 o'clock in the morning I sighted the *Carpathia* on the other side of this great ice pack... between us and the *Titanic*'s position... where I understand he [the *Carpathia*] picked up the boats... I was to the eastward of the position the *Titanic* gave me, but she must have been to the eastward still, because she could not have been through this pack of ice... The *Californian* was there shortly after me...[8]

---

7   American inquiry, p. 764
8   American inquiry, p. 778

By the time of the British enquiry, he had changed his evidence to say that he saw both of these ships shortly before 8 a.m.

The question of the *Californian* aside, although both captains Rostron and Lord testified that they did not come within visual range of each other until 8 a.m., the fact remains that the *Carpathia* had arrived at the *Titanic*'s CQD position at 4 a.m. By the time the first boat was alongside, at 4:10 a.m., it was, according to Rostron, breaking day. At 5 o'clock, it was light enough to see all around the horizon. If, as Moore maintained, he was at the scene at 4:30 a.m., he should have seen the *Carpathia* by 5 a.m., even though she was on the eastern side of a five-to-six mile wide field of ice. That he did not see her until 6 a.m. or 8 a.m, depending on whichever evidence is chosen, can only indicate that Moore was farther to the west than he thought he was and out of visual range.

On the ninth day of the American hearings, Senator Burton put the following to Fourth Officer Boxhall:

> The captain of the *Mount Temple* maintains that the course (sic) as conveyed by the distress signal was wrong; that the *Titanic* was actually eight miles distant from the place indicated. What do you say as to that?

Boxhall replied:

> I do not know what to say. I know our position, because I worked the position out, and I know that it is correct.[9]

---

9   American inquiry, p. 931

He had not been informed of the course, speed, distance, and time run by the *Mount Temple* and had no opportunity to refute Captain Moore's evidence.

All the credible evidence and nautical logic confirm that Fourth Officer Boxhall's CQD position was correct. How then could the *Titanic's* hulk have been found, 73 years later, thirteen miles east of that position?

The answer may lie in oceanic forces.

The *Titanic* sank just south of the Grand Banks of Newfoundland, an area that is influenced by the Gulf Stream, above and below the surface. The Gulf Stream runs east northeast at a rate of 0.5 to 0.8 knots.

Coriolis force, the effect of the earth's rotation on large masses, may have played a role in the final resting site of the *Titanic* by carrying the wreckage eastward. Coriolis force causes a clockwise drift in the northern hemisphere and a counter-clockwise drift in the southern hemisphere, and it exerts a major influence on currents. It exerts such a considerable influence upon the North Atlantic that it causes a slope in the surface of the ocean, which in mid-Atlantic is as much as forty-eight inches above the level of American coastal waters.[10] It would also exert an influence upon a ship the size of the *Titanic*.

It must also be noted that there is no conclusive evidence, nor is there any reason to believe, that the *Titanic* broke in two before she sank. Although several witnesses later claimed that the ship had been severed and that her after-part had settled on the water, others, including Second Officer Lightoller, emphatically denied it. "It is utterly untrue," Lightoller told the British enquiry, "The ship did not and could not have broken in two."[11] The second officer was definitely in a position to know: only

10   Mostert Noel , *Supership*. New York, Alfred A. Knopf, Inc., 1974, p.29
11   British enquiry, 14075

feet away from the sinking ship, he watched her descent "keenly the whole time."[12] In this, Lightoller's testimony was corroborated by Pitman. He, too, denied that the after-part broke off; he was "barely 100 yards away," he testified, and kept his eyes upon her as she went down.[13]

There was also no reason for the hull, which was subjected only to progressive flooding, to break in two. In later years, it was confirmed by ultrasound images that the impact with the ice caused the starboard bow to sustain only a six-slit opening over a length of 100 feet, or about 12 square feet in total. For all intents and purposes, the ultrasound images confirmed the calculation Naval Architect Edward Wilding made in 1912.

An intact hull that has been progressively flooded will most likely have air trapped in many compartments of the ship.[14] Once the ship has lost its stability, there is the further possibility that the hull will turn turtle under the water. This, in turn, will trap air inside the hull. The air will not dissipate until enough depth has been reached for the water pressure to cause the compartments to implode and consequently flood. It can therefore take some time for all buoyancy to be expended and for the ship to finally settle on the ocean floor.

In the *Titanic's* case, it is entirely conceivable that during the time this process was taking place, the submerged hull was drifting eastward with the Gulf Stream underwater currents. Thus, when the hulk finally came to rest upon the ocean floor, the ship was some miles east of Boxhall's CQD position.

---

12 British enquiry, 14094
13 British enquiry, 15076 and 15077
14 Examples of compartments of the ship that are most likely to develop air pockets under the circumstances described above are empty ballast tanks, empty domestic water tanks, engine-room boilers and furnaces, and large refrigerator spaces.

On November 18, 1929, 17 years after the *Titanic* went down, an underwater earthquake of a 7.2 magnitude[15], centred 350 kilometres south of Newfoundland – 100 miles from the position at which the *Titanic*'s wreckage was found – occurred about 20 kilometres below the seabed. This earthquake caused a massive tidal wave, which resulted in death and devastation along the south coast of Newfoundland. The waters receded and the harbours dried up; in no time at all, the tide had reversed and the harbours were flooded. Houses were torn from their foundations and swept out to sea.

Such an underwater force more than likely moved the *Titanic*'s wreckage from its resting place, some miles east of the CQD position, to the one discovered by Dr Ballard. It might also account for the fact the *Titanic*'s hull is now broken up and scattered over the ocean floor.

Fourth Officer Boxhall never wavered in his assertion that his distress position was correct. He stood by it during the inquiries and defended it throughout his later life. When he died in April 1967, at the age of 83, at his request his cremated remains were scattered at sea – over latitude 41° 46′ N, longitude 50° 14′ W.

Navigational confirmation of Titanic's CQD position

Navigational calculations, based on the evidence, confirm that Boxhall's CQD position, of 41° 46′ N, 50° 14′ W, was correct.

---

15 Anderson, Thane, et al. "Paleoenvironmental Evidence for the 1929 Tidal Wave (Tsunami) Disaster in South Burin Peninsula, Newfoundland."
(www.cciw.ca/ eman-temp/reports/meetings/national96/andersont.html.)

By examining the evidence of the *Titanic*'s navigating officers on April 14, 1912, we can determine the noon 14th position.

Mr Lowe: [...]. We are there to do the navigating part so the senior officer can be and will be in full charge of the bridge and have nothing to worry his head about. We have all that, the junior officers; there are four of us. The three seniors are in absolute charge of the boat. They have nothing to worry themselves about. They simply have to walk backward and forward and look after the ship, and we do all the figuring and all that sort of thing in our chart room.

Junior (Navigating) Officers on watch Sunday, April 14, 1912:

8 a.m. – 12 noon   Fourth Officer Boxhall, Sixth Officer Moody (Sixth Officer Moody, lost with the ship)

12 noon – 4 p.m.   Third Officer Pitman, Fifth Officer Lowe

4 p.m. – 6 p.m.   Fourth Officer Boxhall, Sixth Officer Moody

6 p.m. – 8 p.m.   Third Officer Pitman, Fifth Officer Lowe

8 p.m. – 12 midnight   Fourth Officer Boxhall, Sixth Officer Moody

Senator Smith: Did you have any part in determining the course and position of the *Titanic* on Sunday afternoon and evening?

Mr Lowe: I worked the course from noon until what we call the "corner"; that is, 42 north, 47 west. I really forget the course now. It is 60° 33½' west – that is as near as I can remember – and 162 miles to the corner.

This evidence of Fifth Officer Lowe was given on April 24, ten days after the accident. Without the benefit of charts, log books, or sight books, all of which were lost with the ship, he was questioned on the navigation of the ship.

Third Officer Pitman, as noted above, was on watch with Mr Lowe. He stated:

> (A.) [...]. I thought that the course should have been altered at 5 p.m. (Q.) Why did you think so? – (A.) Judging from the distance run from noon.

Accepting "60° 33½' west" as S 60° 33½' W true and rejecting "and 162 miles to the corner," which is obviously the distance run from noon to evening civil twilight for stellar observation, and accepting Third Officer Pitman's evidence ("I thought that the course should have been altered at 5 p.m... Judging from the distance run from noon"), we can calculate as follows:

Working back from the expected alter course
position at the "corner" 42° N and 47° W
applying 5 hrs x 22.1* knots = 110.5 miles,
makes noon 14th position 42° 54.3′ N, 44°
50′ W.

The course being steered was S 85° W [S 62° W true].
Corroborating this, is the evidence of Quartermaster Rowe.

QM Rowe:

17587.   What course was she steering? – S 85° W.

17588.   By the compass in front of you, I suppose? – By
the steering compass.

At 5:45 or 5:50 p.m., the course was altered to N 71°W
compass.

QM Rowe:

17583.   During that watch, did you alter the course at any
time? – Yes.

17584.   Do you remember when it was? – Yes, at 5:45.

17590.   At 5:45 to what did you alter it? – N 71° W.

17586.   Now, before you altered course, do you remember
what course your vessel was steering? – Yes.

17587.   What course was she steering? – S 85° W.

At British Enquiry 15315, Fourth Officer Boxhall, in
answer to the question, "Between 4 and 6, while you were
on watch, do you remember the course being altered?"
answered, "The course was altered at 5:50."

15316.   Do you remember what it was altered to? – I do
not remember the compass course, but I
remember the true course was S 86° W.

There is a plausible reason for the five-minute discrepancy (5:45 p.m. as opposed to 5:50 p.m.) in the time the course was altered. The course change was made from the standard compass by one of the on-watch junior officers – positioned between numbered two and three funnels; Quartermaster Rowe, at the helm, was responsible for bringing the ship to the required course by order of the junior officer. QM Rowe would have noted the time as 5:45 p.m. when he commenced the alteration, whereas junior officer Boxhall would have entered into the log book record 5:50 p.m. as the time when the steering compass had settled on the new course.

As Charles H. Lightoller stated on Day five to the U.S. Senate Inquiry:

> "We have a standard compass and a steering compass. The standard compass is the compass we go by. That is the course that is handed over from one senior officer to another, the standard course. The junior officer goes to the standard compass which is connected with the wheelhouse by a bell, or by a bell push, wire and bell, and when she is on her course he rings that bell continually, showing the ship is on her course with the standard compass.
>
> The other officer takes her head inside the wheelhouse from the compass the quartermaster is steering by. The standard course is on a board and the steering compass course is also on a board. Therefore, the quartermaster uses the board that is there for the steering compass. The senior officer of the watch looks to the standard compass board and passes that course along."

In the 6 to 8 p.m. last dog watch, it was the duty of the junior watch officer to prepare the information for evening stellar observation, i.e., time of civil twilight, stars available with approximate azimuths and altitudes. Junior watch officer Lowe determined evening civil twilight to be 22:21 GMT – noon transit (Sun) 15:00 GMT = 7 hrs 21 mins x 22 kts** = 162 miles. This is most likely what Lowe meant, when he answered from memory, that the distance was 162 miles – the distance run from noon to civil twilight for stellar observation.

Mr Lowe: I worked the course from noon until what we call the "corner", that is 42 north, 47 west. I really forget the course now. It is 60° 33½′ west – that is as near as I can remember – and 162 miles to the corner.

From noon position 14th, 42° 54.3′ N, 44° 50′ W.
Course S 62° W (242° T) to 5:45 p.m. = 5 hrs 45 mins
22 kts = 126.5 miles
Gives a/c position 41° 54.9′ N, 47° 20.8′ W.

5:45 p.m. a/c to **S 86° W (266° T)** to stellar observation
= 1 hr 36 mins =
@ 22 kts = 35.2 miles gives position 41° 52.4′ N, 48° 07.8′ W.
distance run from noon 126.5+35.2 =161.7 **(162)** miles.

Course 266° T from stellar observation to 11:40 p.m. =
4 hrs 19 mins
@ 22 kts = 95 miles gives CQD position
41° 45.8′ N, 50° 14.5′ W **(41° 46′ N. 50° 14′ W)**.

Course 266° T from 5:45 p.m. to 11:40 p.m. = 5 hrs 55
mins
@ 22 kts = 130 miles gives CQD position
41° 45.8′ N, 50° 14.3′ W **(41° 46′ N, 50° 14′ W)**.

Therefore, *Titanic*'s CQD position was correct. The wreck
site, located by Dr Robert Ballard, is 099° True. distance
13 nautical miles, from her CQD position.

---

*   Memorandum of Mr. Pitman
**   162 miles/7 hrs 21 mins = 22.04 kts.

CONCLUSION

...the armchair complaint is a common disease, and generally accepted as one of the necessary evils from which the seafarer is condemned to suffer.

— *Commander Charles Herbert Lightoller*

My fascination with ships and ice came at an early age. I was born in the seaport of Carmanville, on the northeast coast of Newfoundland, where, from December to June of each year, floes and icebergs are abundant as they float past the rocky coast en route to a southern destination.

My father and grandfather were master mariners, and while I was growing up, my only ambition was to be a master mariner too. Pictures and stories of large ships, such as the *Titanic*, the *Queen Mary*, and the *Queen Elizabeth*, captivated me. Of them all, the legend of the *Titanic* and the tragedy that ensued on the night of April 14, 1912, held the most sway: how was it possible, I wondered, for such a large and stately ship to "run into an iceberg" in unlimited visibility, even at night?

From the time of my first voyage in 1953, as a young deck officer navigating through the ice-infested waters of Newfoundland's eastern coast, every iceberg was a reminder of the *Titanic*'s fateful voyage. Still the question remained unanswered, nibbling at my subconscious for decades to come.

By the 1970s I had acquired extensive experience in ice navigation. This experience, combined with my master foreign-going certificate of competency, enabled me to reach some conclusions about what had happened that night.

It was obvious to me that the inquiries' assessors – or their technical advisers – did not comprehend the hydrodynamic reactions of vessels when under way. If they had, they would not have accepted without question the premise that the *Titanic* had hit an iceberg.

Years later, after I'd had the opportunity to study the transcripts, it became equally clear to me that a crucial bit of evidence had been misinterpreted. Fleet and Lee's assertion that they had seen haze, when atmospheric conditions that night precluded the possibility, was dismissed by the inquiries as a fabrication to cover up the lookouts' late warning. Yet this "haze", I am convinced, is the key to understanding what happened that night.

It is highly unlikely that the lookouts would have mistaken an iceberg for haze. It is, however, entirely conceivable that men not professionally trained would mistake a strip of pack ice, some four to five miles distant, for haze. I have no doubt that Fleet and Lee's haze was exactly that: a strip of pack ice, which was probably no more than a quarter of a mile wide and largely composed of multi-year ice and growlers, the hardest type of ice imaginable and the most difficult type to navigate.

If Fleet and Lee had been instructed to notify the bridge upon sighting anything unusual, it stands to reason they would have informed the bridge of their sighting of the "haze." First Officer Murdoch could then have taken immediate action. But the duty of keeping a safe lookout should not have been left to those in the crow's nest. They alone were not responsible for being the "eyes of the ship." The ultimate responsibility of keeping an effective lookout belonged to the bridge personnel. It was incumbent upon the bridge watch officers, and particularly the officer in charge, to be acutely aware at all times of anything that could threaten the safe navigation of the ship. As the senior officer on the bridge, Murdoch ought to have seen as soon as the lookouts, if not sooner, the dark shadow on the horizon they tragically mistook for haze.

By the time the ice was recognized for what it was, the *Titanic* was almost on top of it. With only seconds to go before impact, Murdoch had no time to take evasive action. The collision was inevitable, but the damage would have been minimized had the ship entered the ice on a straight course instead of at an angle. In any event, the rudder should have been kept amidship, which would have allowed the stem bar and both the port and starboard entrance bow plates to equally absorb the impact of the ice. If this had been done, the *Titanic* certainly would not have sustained the damage she did sustain, with the resultant loss of life. If, on the other hand, the ship had indeed collided with an iceberg, the effect of that collision would have been immediate and deadly. The crew would not have been able to launch lifeboats and send distress signals, and it is doubtful that anyone on board would have survived.

There are few accidents that are truly unavoidable. Most are a result of human error, of a temporary lapse in judgment, and the *Titanic* tragedy is no exception. But in reviewing the events of that April 14 and attempting to explain what went wrong and how, the events must be viewed with clarity, not clouded by emotion or shaped by a desire to find an easy scapegoat.

The lookouts' late warning and the bridge's failure to keep a safe watch were perhaps the most crucial elements in the loss of the ship and the death of almost 1500 people. They were not, however, the only elements.

There was also the message that was never passed to the bridge. If Captain Smith and his senior officers had received the report from the *Mesaba*, warning of ice in latitude 42° N to 41° 25′ N, longitude 49° W to 50° 30′ W, Smith could have altered his course even further to pass well south of the ice field. The collision with the ice would never have occurred. Instead, because the *Mesaba*'s wireless operator failed to prioritize the message with the code "MSG", which indicated a personal message for the recipient ship's captain, and because the *Titanic*'s wireless operator was preoccupied with sending the passengers' personal messages[1], the ice warning was not delivered and Smith continued unknowingly on his course.

Then, too, were the out-of-date Board of Trade regulations on the number of lifeboats a vessel was required to carry. Because the regulations based the required number on a vessel's gross tonnage, the *Titanic*'s lifeboat count was well within regulation. It was nevertheless totally inadequate for the number of people she had on board. If there had been a place in a lifeboat for every person the *Titanic* carried, the death toll resulting from the sinking would have been greatly diminished, if not entirely negligible.

The lack of lifeboat drills, as well, contributed to the magnitude of the tragedy. Proper training would not only have ensured that the lifeboats were filled quickly and in an orderly fashion, it would also have provided instruction to the crew on the capacity of each lifeboat. The fact that there were enough lifeboats for only about half on board

---

1   British enquiry, pp. 371, 576, 715

was made worse by the fact that many of the lifeboats left with less than a full load. The limitations placed on survival by not enough lifeboats were therefore lowered even further by some of the boats leaving half empty.

In assessing what contributed to the *Titanic* disaster, however, it is just as important to assess what was not a factor. Into the latter category fall the two captains – Smith of the *Titanic*, Lord of the *Californian* – both of whom were, in one fashion or another, held accountable by the public for the loss of so many lives.

Even though the British enquiry exonerated him, Captain Smith's memory has been damaged by the accusations that he was speeding through ice-infested waters in an attempt to make a record crossing. The allegations are unfounded. The *Titanic* was not speeding; her engines were not even fully opened up. Smith maintained his speed, it is true, as he neared areas in which ice could be encountered, but in doing so did what almost every sea captain has done before and since. As an experienced mariner, he would have known that in good visibility ice can be seen in time to take evasive action. Not only that, but as far as he was concerned, ice posed no immediate threat to his ship. By holding his course for almost an hour beyond the turning point, he believed he had passed south of all reported ice. The one message that would have told him otherwise he never received.

Captain Lord was not a party to the *Titanic* tragedy, but he spent a lifetime trying to clear his name. In the 92 years since the sinking, he has been regarded by many as the captain who slept while the *Titanic* went down. His censure grew out of the allegation that the *Californian* and the *Titanic* were within sight of each other while the *Titanic* was sinking, that the sinking ship's distress signals were clearly visible to those on the *Californian*, and that he turned a blind eye to the crisis, choosing not to come to the *Titanic's* rescue when the lives of so many were held in the balance. Yet the facts tell a different story. It is obvious from the testimony presented at the subsequent inquiries that the two vessels were not within viewing distance of each other. The *Titanic's* navigating lights, deck lights, and Morse lights could not have been seen from the deck of the *Californian* any more than the *Californian's* lights could have been seen from the deck of the *Titanic*. Since the two ships were more than 16 miles apart during the times in question, their lights were outside both the geographic range and the luminous range. Moreover, the ship that the *Titanic's* Fourth Officer Boxhall reported seeing from his deck came from the westward, whereas the *Californian* was then to the northward of the *Titanic*. And although it is quite likely that the rockets viewed by those on the *Californian* came from the *Titanic*, Lord did have reason to believe that they were company signals, sent up by an unknown ship that was in the *Californian's* line of sight. Lord's transgression that night was in not verifying for himself what it was his crew members were witnessing; he cannot be faulted for not steaming to the rescue of a ship that showed no signs of being in distress and later steamed away from him.

Controversy has dogged the sinking of the *Titanic* ever since the tragedy was made known on April 15, 1912, and it likely will for some years to come. Few human events have stirred the imagination, incited the pathos, and had such a hold upon the western world. Decades later, the story continues to captivate new generations, as it did the old. Books have been written, movies produced, web sites spawned, each adding a different perspective but perpetuating the myths. The story will be told again and again, but in the telling the myths must be laid to rest – or our historic link will be lost forever.

ACKNOWLEDGEMENTS

I am grateful to the many people who have assisted me in the writing of this book.

Many thanks to Ms Kim Todd-Finn, for starting me off on the right track, and Mr Barry LeDrew, for helping me choose my publisher.

I also owe a debt of gratitude to Dr Jacek Pawlowski, former director of the Centre for Marine Simulation; Captain Douglas G. Skinner, Simulation and Navigation Instructor, School of Maritime Studies of Memorial University; and Captain Frank Wheeler, School of Maritime Studies of Memorial University – all of whom provided advice and encouragement throughout this endeavour.

As well, my research was greatly facilitated by the assistance of: Captain C.L. Ball, former director of operations of the Atlantic Pilotage Authority, in obtaining for me, through Dalhousie University of Halifax and Memorial University of Newfoundland, a copy of the official transcripts of the British enquiry into the sinking of *RMS Titanic*; Ms Heather Wareham, archivist, Maritime History Archive of Memorial University, in acquiring for me the official transcripts of the American Senate inquiry into the sinking of *RMS Titanic*; meteorologist Bruce Whiffen, for patiently answering my questions on climatic conditions and causes; veteran sealing captain Morrisey Johnson, for sharing his insight into seal harvesting from the Newfoundland ice floes; Captain Peter Smith, for allowing me to use his vast marine library; and the St. John's, Newfoundland harbour pilots, for their unfailing support and obtaining for me difficult-to-find charts.

I must also thank marine pilots Captains M. J. Furlong, Edward Anthony, Nelson Pitman, Donald MacAlpine, and Terrence Ricketts, and former ship masters Captains Tom Sellers, Denis Drown, Henry Flight, and Joseph Prim, for their welcome feedback on the completed manuscript.

And finally, the writing of this book was greatly facilitated by the computer lessons of my grandson, Gregory Collins, who taught me the difference between a cursor and a mouse.

BIBLIOGRAPHY

Anderson, Thane, et al. *Paleoenvironmental Evidence for the 1929 Tidal Wave (Tsunami) Disaster in South Burin Peninsula, Newfoundland.*
Internet: http://www.cciw.ca/emantemp/reports/meetings/national96/andersont.html

Barnaby, K.C. *Some Ship Disasters and their Causes.* New Jersey: A.S. Barnes and Company, Inc., 1970.

Bowditch, Nathaniel, LL.D. (1773–1838), *The American Practical Navigator.* Maryland: Defense Mapping Agency Hydrographic/Topographic Center, 1995.

Eaton, John P. and Charles A. Haas. *Titanic: Destination Disaster. The Legends and the Reality.* New York: W.W. Norton & Company, Inc., 1987.

Lloyd's Weekly Shipping Index, April 1912.

Lloyd's Weekly Shipping Index, May 1912.

Minutes of Evidence of the Enquiry into the Loss of the S.S. "Titanic". Wreck Commissioners' Court, Scottish Hall, Buckingham Gate, 1912.

Mostert, Noel. *Supership*. New York: Alfred A. Knopf, Inc., 1974.

Report on the Loss of the S.S. Titanic: The Official Government Enquiry. New York: St. Martin's Press, 1998.

Official Transcripts of the "Titanic" Disaster Hearings. Subcommittee of the Committee on Commerce, United States Senate, Sixty-Second Congress, Second Session.

Winocour, Jack, ed. *The Story of the Titanic as Told by Its Survivors Lawrence Beesley, Archibald Gracie, Commander Lightoller, Harold Bride*. New York: Dover Publications, Inc., 1960.

GLOSSARY

ABAFT – towards the stern of the ship, relative to some other object or position.

ABEAM – on a bearing or direction at right-angles from the fore and aft line, outwards from the widest part of the ship.

BACK STAYS – any of various shrouds forming part of a vessel's standing rigging and leading aft from the masts above a lower mast to the sides or stern of the vessel in order to reinforce the masts against forward pull.

BERNOULLI EFFECT (INTERACTION) – hydraulics. The decrease in pressure as the velocity of a fluid increases.

CENTRE LINE (FORE AND AFT LINE) – an imaginary line passing from the stem to the stern through the centre of the vessel.

CQD – Morse code signal signifying DISTRESS, later changed to SOS.

CROW'S NEST, (*Titanic*) – a lookout cage, constructed of steel fitted on the foremast at a height of about 95 feet above the water line.

GROWLER – smaller piece of ice than a bergy bit or floeberg, often transparent but appearing green or almost black in color, extending less than 1 m above sea surface and normally occupying an area of about 20 sq.m.

HEAD REACH – the distance along the projection of the original track that a ship travels before coming to rest, after the astern order is given.

HELM – another name for the tiller, by which the rudder of small vessels, such as yachts and lifeboats, etc. is swung, and also the general term associated with orders connected with the steering of a ship[...].

For some three centuries all helm orders given in ships remained applicable to the tiller, and an order from the navigator of a ship to a helmsman of, for example, "port 200 meant that the helmsman put the wheel over to 200 to starboard, the equivalent direction of moving the tiller 200 port, and the rudder and the ship's head moved to starboard.

This practice was universal until after the First World War (1914–1918), when some nations began the practice of relating helm orders to the rudder and no longer the tiller, so that an order of, for instance, "starboard 200 meant turning the wheel, the rudder, and the ship's head all to starboard. By the mid 1930s all maritime nations had adopted this practice, which removed the anomaly of a navigator giving the order "port" when he wanted to turn the ship to starboard, and vice-versa.

HUMMOCKED ICE – sea ice piled haphazardly one piece over another to form an uneven surfaced.

HYDRODYNAMICS – the mathematical science that deals with fluids and bodies moving through fluids.

ICEBERG – a massive piece of ice of greatly varying shape, more than 5 m above sea level, which has broken away from a glacier.

PACK ICE – term used in a wide sense to include any area of sea ice, other than fast ice, no matter what form it takes or how it is disposed.

PIVOT POINT – the point about which a ship actually turns. The point is transient and is not the same as the center of gravity.

QUICK WATER FLOW – the flow water resulting from the propeller turning.

WEIGH ANCHOR – to heave up a ship's anchor in preparation for getting underway.

STRIP – long narrow area of pack ice, about 1 km or less in width.

TURN TURTLE – naut. To capsize or turn over completely in foundering.

TILLER – a wood or metal bar which fits into or round the head of the rudder and by which the rudder is moved as required.